AFLOAT ON THE DUTCH WATERWAYS

As seen from the deck of a Linssen

Written and illustrated
by
Shirley Faure

With grateful thanks to all who have helped to make this book possible:

to my husband who provided the comfortable comfortable floating studio upon which so many illustrations were produced, and patiently encouraged me along the way; to Peter Linssen for his support and enthusiasm from the start of the project; to Paul Beelen for his advice and assistance on final presentation; to the staff at Linssen Yachts; to Liza Copeland for comments and amendments, and to all those we met upon the waters who gave their time and suggestions so willingly.

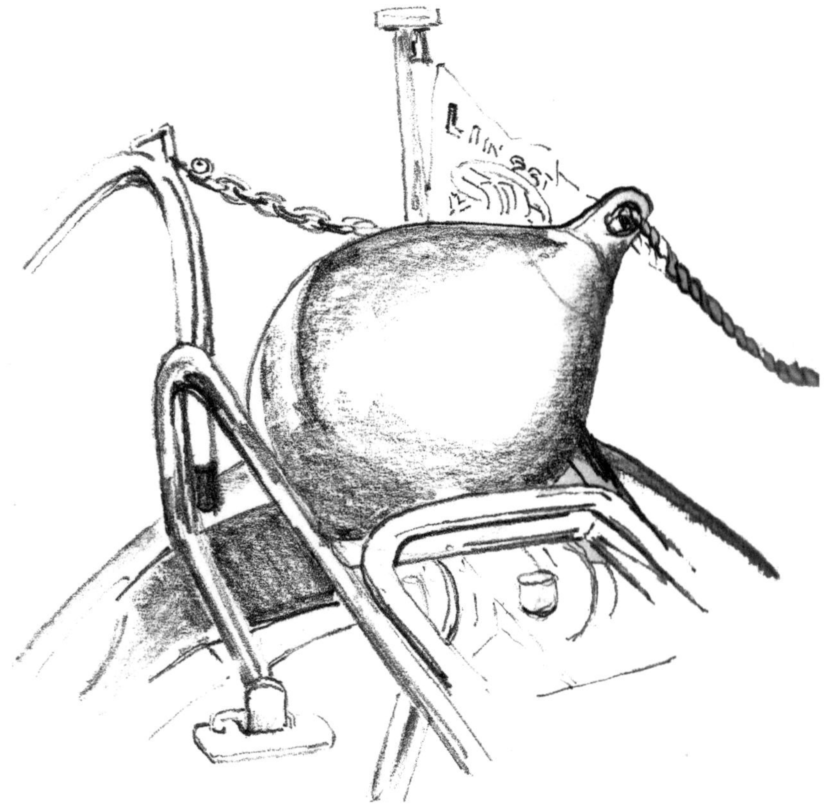

Published 2008 by Shirley Faure
jhfaure@tiscali.co.uk
www.artist-afloat.com

A catalogue record for this book is available from the British Library.
ISBN 978-0-9557486-0-8

Printed in Belgium

Reproduction of the illustrations on pages 29 and 39 is by kind permission of the owners of the original watercolour paintings.

Our sailing days were over...........

we came to seek the perfect "**Yachtsman's Motor Boat**"

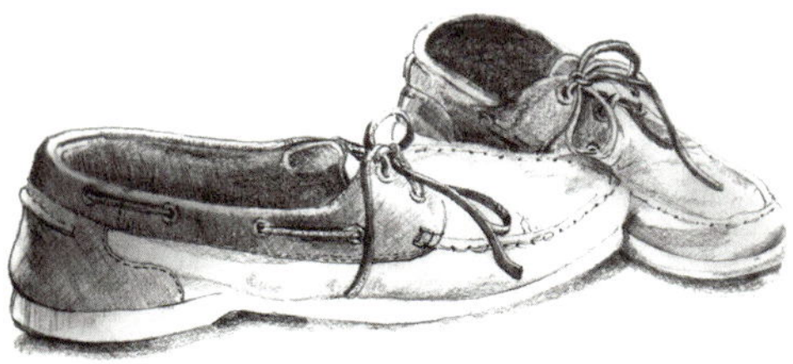

Our journey through the canals of Holland began in the south, at Maasbracht in the Limburg region. We came here to visit the manufacturing facilities of the Linssen range of steel motor yachts. Three generations of this family and their craftsmen work together to create a fine range of comfortable cruisers. Customers may choose a specification to suit their own particular requirements. Gleaming new models filled the showroom. A range of used boats for sale filled their marina.

What better way could we choose to travel at a leisurely speed through the waterways of Europe? When travelling at perhaps 5-6 knots there would be time for an artist to sketch the passing scene. Sometimes time would permit a more detailed study. So we came to buy a Dutch Sturdy 380.

I will share some of my impressions with you...

LINSSE

It was a new challenge when we bought our first steel motor yacht for we had long been sailors enjoying competitive racing in the tropical waters of Malaysia and Singapore.

Now we had to forget about sail trimming, reefing down in a gale, cooking meals at an angle of 45 degrees, the excitement of the chase, and learn the rules for navigation, customs and courtesy adopted on quiet inland waters.

The Maas

We made our way across the Channel to take delivery of the new motor yacht named 'FOLEO' and set off, not without trepidation, to clear the deep lock at Sluis Heel and to begin our exploration of Europe in the slow lane as we saw it "from the deck of a Linssen".

All journeys from Maasbracht start on the river Maas. One can choose to go south to Maastricht or to follow the river downstream in a northerly direction. There is also an option to take the Wessem-Nederweert then Zuid-Willemsvaart canals and enter Belgian waters, or to continue on to perhaps Eindhoven or 's Hertogenbosch on a less used waterway with a number of locks which slow the progress but make a pleasing diversion away from commercial traffic.

Looking back at Sluis Heel, the first lock – a drop in level of 8-9 metres down the River Maas

Read on and join us as we begin our travels

It can be hard work keeping 19 tons of steel boat close to the lock side in turbulent water.

Do not fear!
It all becomes easy with experience!
Sluis Heel is user friendly for there are plenty of sliding bollards which rise up or drop as the lock levels change – once positioned no moving of warps is necessary.

That very first lock with a new boat can be a daunting experience! It is best to keep her as close to the lock side as possible – the wash caused by a few inconsiderate barge owners using maximum thrust to move quickly out of the lock can cause such turbulence that in a small boat one is made to feel like laundry in a washing machine!

The first rule one must learn is that pleasure boats give way at all times to working barges.

Sliding bollard at Sluis Heel

Fishermen at Roermond

When the lock gates open one is free to move out as soon as commercial traffic has gone. These reaches of the Maas in Limburg are pleasantly rural, popular with local fishermen who sit motionless on the banks for hours on end.

Huge flocks of geese can always be seen, fighting over territory and noisily defending their own.

The Maas (Meuse) is one of the 3 great rivers of Holland, leading eventually into the Hollands Diep and the delta. It carries considerable barge traffic but despite this it is delightfully rural. Often cows come down to the water's edge to drink and then seek shade under the great trees. Fields are alive with flocks of breeding geese, swans and water fowl.. There are recurrent sandy bays formed naturally between stone breakwaters. These are greatly enjoyed in summer when levels are low by the owners of small motor boats who are able to land on a seemingly isolated and private beach. Several areas of these man made lakes where gravel and sand have been removed, are now landscaped and naturalised, set aside as reserves for wild life, and shared with all who use the river for recreational enjoyment.

The Maas

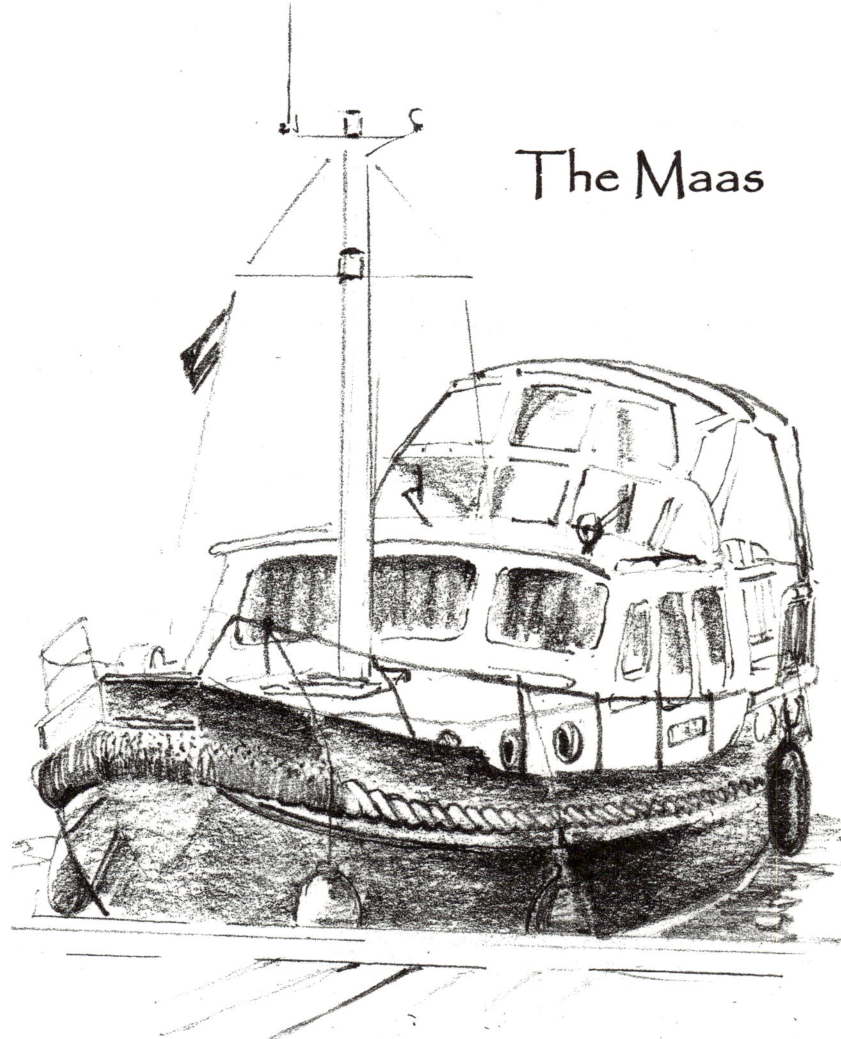

Marinas have been built in many of these lakes where one can rest awhile with all facilities to hand. Often we choose to drop anchor alone for the night, watch the setting sun, and wake next morning to glorious calm solitude interrupted only by the sound of the dawn chorus.

Page from my sketchbook

Springtime on the Maas

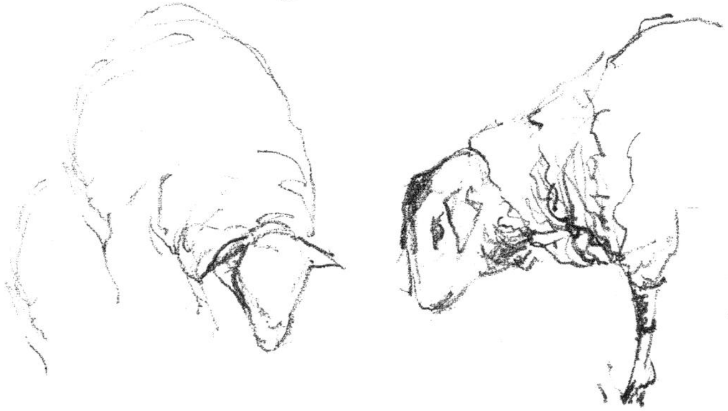

New life was plentiful in the fields bordering the Maas in early Spring.

The Limburg region has a different character from much of Holland. As the borders of both Belgium and Germany are so close, it is natural that architectural features should be evident in this. The countryside is green and wooded, and the frequency of that symbol of Holland, the windmill, is much less evident. One such, however, the Grauwe Beer, is visible from the river as one moves downstream.

The Maas in Limburg

Behind this group of houses lies the castle of Kessel – a strategically placed defence overlooking the Maas. It was used as an ammunition store during the last war. The retreating German troops blew up the keep. Restoration has not yet been undertaken.

'Passantenhaven' – mooring facilities for a short stay during daylight hours are offered by many of the towns and villages, enabling visitors to go ashore, buy provisions or take a meal. These can be subject to uncomfortable wash from passing commercial traffic and one should not stay long.

More and more small marinas have been provided, such as this one at Kessel, which offer facilities to ensure a peaceful night of rest off the river, with perhaps the luxury of power and water at hand, often a simple restaurant and the chance to meet with other watersport enthusiasts.

Intrigued by some ruins on the bank above the passantenhaven at Arcen, we went ashore to investigate. A well displayed tablet showed that archaeological excavations had revealed remains on the site dating back many centuries. In times past the tower had been part of a toll house erected to take money from traders using the river.

The 'passantenhaven' (short stay jetty) in Cuijk enabled me to make a quick sketch of a portion of Martinus Kerk. We learned of a bridge built in Roman times across the Maas at this point, but of this we could find no trace. The bridge gave the Roman inhabitants control over the road between Nijmegen and Maastricht. How strange there was a bridge in ancient times yet not today!

Arcen – the old toll house

The Maas

Leaving the town of Cuijk with its impressive church that dominates the river scene, one may choose to continue downstream towards the North Sea, or take the short Maas-Waal Canal north to the town of Nijmegen, thence on to the Rhine, perhaps following this great river to Cologne, or heading north to Zwolle and Groningen down the River IJssel and the Noord-Willemskanaal.

Ravenstein

The Maas

Friend at the helm

This time we follow the course of the Maas downstream, the river turns west, widens, but continues to present a delightfully rural character. We enjoyed pleasant halts at both Ravenstein and Batenburg.

Batenburg

Bergse Maas

Further downstream the Maas becomes the Bergse Maas. Heusden is a favoured stopover. Although a modern marina exists, some, like us, prefer to creep carefully through the narrow opening under the pedestrian lift bridge into the inner harbour, from which one may climb to the cobbled streets of this delightful fortified stronghold town. So attractive are the surroundings, old houses preserved from centuries past, some rebuilt in original style after the ravages of World War II, working mills (3), the ramparts, the market square and the Vismarkt that several pages of my sketchbooks have been filled with memories. How fortunate that those residents protested 50 years ago and refused to accept modern planning in place of their heritage. There's room for this, but not, we feel, in this historic town.

A settlement on the bank of the Maas at Heusden has been traced back to the C13. Much can be read of the long history of occupation, flood and disaster. In the early years of the 80 Years War (1568-1648), the town was occupied by the Spaniards. However the people of the town chose to ally with William of Orange. Noting the strategic position of Heusden, he ordered fortifications to be built around the site of an earlier castle stronghold. Moats were dug in 1579, and ramparts and defences soon followed.

Heusden

By the early C19 much of this work had fallen into disrepair and was dismantled. Following discovery of a map drawn in 1649 by Willem Blaeu, a renowned cartographer, a restoration based on lines then drawn was undertaken in 1968. Today we can all walk again on the ramparts, stroll along cobbled streets and enjoy the town in company with some of the 350,000 tourists said to visit each year.

Bergse Maas - Heusden

Heusden – detail of a window in the market square.

At one time in its history this 'binnenhaven' had been filled in. How grateful we are today that this charming feature has been re-instated.

A complicated wooden stairway leads from the restored quayside up to the Vismarkt and the cobbled streets of this well preserved town. Much of the original fortification remains, although the former ramparts are, today, covered with grass. Three post mills are kept in good repair, and occasionally when the wind is right the sails are unfurled and visitors invited to see the workings within.

Anchors

Prominently carried before an old sailing barge in the historic harbour at Woudrichem is this elegant example.

This classic anchor was securely fastened to the railings along the pontoon in Goes – although it would have been a heavy souvenir to lift!

Alongside our mooring in Dordrecht we noted another classic example on a neighbouring boat from a previous century.

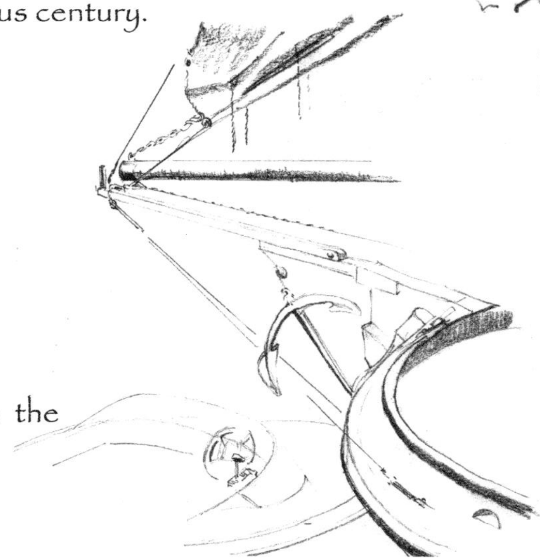

Heavy Admiralty type anchor rests on the quayside at Maastricht.

This one lay on the quay beside the harbour office in Nieuwe Haven Dordrecht

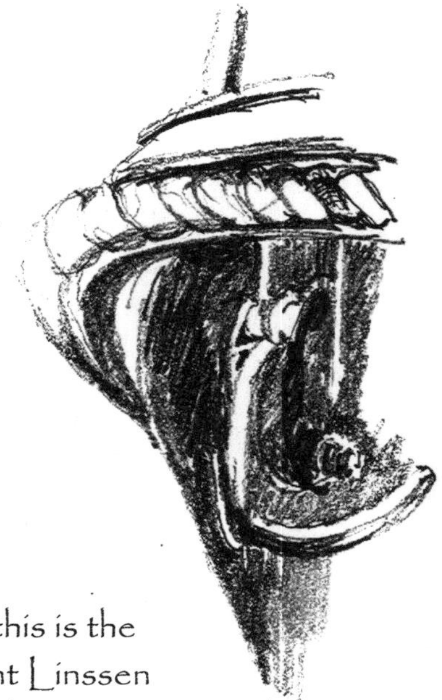

And this is the current Linssen example, a modern galvanized steel Bruce anchor particularly suited for use in muddy estuaries.

Many of us think of the windmill as an iconic symbol of Holland. More than 1,000 mills remain to this day, and form a distinctive feature of the often flat landscape.

It is interesting to learn that there is a 'language of the mills'. When the sails rest in the true vertical and horizontal, this means it is ready to operate. However, on a polder mill, stationary sails set at a cross means it is firmly at rest. An upper sail set to the right of vertical (remember all sails move in an anticlockwise direction) can be read as a sign of some celebration, and one with sails to the left denotes a mourning.

Mill on the Kaageplassen

Construction methods vary – some are built on a base of brick or stone, others mainly of wood. These are frequently painted green with white edging. Often the rotating cap is neatly thatched. The windshaft (point where the sails cross) is usually painted red, and maybe you will note a sign beneath which gives the name of the mill and date of its building.

The builder of this hollow post mill in Meerkerk has created space for living accommodation below for the operator.

The first windmills to be used in Holland date back to the mid C13. Designs vary considerably, but essentially mills fall into one of several recognisable types suited to their purpose. Polder mills were used for drainage, whereas industrial mills specialised in grinding corn, hulling rice, crushing oilseeds and as saw mills. Different methods are used to turn the sails into the wind. Post mills turn in full, a tall pole joined to a post connects to a wheel enabling the operator to turn the sails in any direction to make use of the optimum wind.

A stage mill, such as this one in Meppel, operates in the same way, but the post comes just to balcony level – only the top half will turn which is useful when the mill is built near surrounding buildings.

Leaving the main course of the Maas we headed north to reach the second of the three great rivers that feed into the Delta – the Waal (Rhine). Some of its mighty power had already been diverted into distributaries, but still here the current runs at speed, and we welcomed a diversion into the sheltered harbour of Woudrichem – one of living history.

The Waal - Woudrichem

Decorated with pots and baskets of geraniums glowing with the red of high summer, and strung with lines of washing drying in the breeze, we found a group of large century old wooden sailing barges, their inhabitants a small community living in a simple way little changed by the progress of time. We then noticed a group of small 7-8' long dark stained fishing boats with half formed cuddies and oversized leeboards raised from the water – we believe a local craft but not observed by us before. A jetty conveniently placed enabled us to stay a short while and enjoy the restful scene.

A pleasant stop can be made at Meerkerk, where moorings are provided along the banks near the mill for the use of passing craft.

The skipper, relaxed, at the helm.

Merwede Canal

A welcome change of tempo came as we left the fast flowing Waal and turned into the lock leading to the Merwede canal. This winds through the pastoral countryside of mid-Holland to emerge on the third of the great rivers, the Lek. The banks of the canal are higher than the fields, lined to one side with carpets of ox-eye daisies and buttercups and to the other with meadowsweet and bramble, broken by brilliant patches of yellow iris. How strange that the flora should be so different just yards apart – doubtless due to the scattering of seed by the prevailing wind.

As we near the end of the Merwede canal the industrial areas return. We must clear the lock to bring us out into the busy waters of the Amsterdam-Rhine canal. The water here is frequently churned to a fierce maelstrom by passing barges hurrying upstream to the industrial towns of Germany, or down to the port of Amsterdam. The banks are solid walls of concrete and wash is given no chance to dissipate before it returns to confuse the water even more, unlike the upstream areas where natural banks interchange with sandy beaches contained within frequent breakwaters that serve to minimise the effect of current and turbulence.

We could follow this wide canal directly to Amsterdam, but instead choose to divert into the calm winding passage of the River Vecht, formerly the main water route to Amsterdam. In 1952 the Amsterdam-Rhine canal was opened, and the river became once more a peaceful rural area.

Amsterdam-Rhine Canal into River Vecht

It is always with a sense of relief that we make the sharp turn through a narrow opening into the river Vecht. Bordered by stately mansions, some still privately owned, each turn of the river brings new delightful sights. Many of these large houses were built by the 17 wealthy original members of the Dutch East India company. Profits made in a former age allowed a standard of living which few can enjoy today.

Our first stop on the river alongside the quay at Maarsen.

The River Vecht

Moorings on the banks of the Vecht at Maarssen are popular with summer visitors – arrive early to avoid a long walk back to town for dinner.

All larger craft on the river must wait for the lock keepers to stop the road traffic and raise the lift bridges. A charge for this service is made – at each bridge an operator will swing a clog suspended on a fishing line into the cockpit, expecting the crew to insert the appropriate toll quickly whilst passing. Occasionally this fails and with regret one hears a splash as a crew member mistimes his payment. No time to reverse – the bridge must re-open. Doubtless the river is dredged from time to time and treasure reclaimed!

Loosdrecht

Passing through one of three possible locks off the River Vecht, one can enter the Loosdrechtse Plassen – set amongst fertile arable land, an area of 8,900 acres has become a popular site for water sports, crowded in summer time with enthusiastic sailors and amply well supplied with clubs and marinas. The lakes are not a natural feature of this area – they have derived from flooded peat workings dating back to the C14.

Of course there were many traditional modern yachts, dinghies and other craft around, but as an artist I was seeking to draw those more appealing and unusual to an English eye!

Dutch schouw in Loosdrecht

Back on the Vecht again, we cruise gently downstream, stopping here and there to visit a farm for supplies of cheese, to buy fresh bread or to enjoy a meal ashore. The scenery gradually changes as we near the town of Muiden which will mark our entry into the IJsselmeer. Houseboats line the banks, some elaborate and comfortable with designer floating gardens, worthy of an English Chelsea Flower Show medal, containing trellis, water features, decorative stone beds, fountains and even statues.

The River Vecht

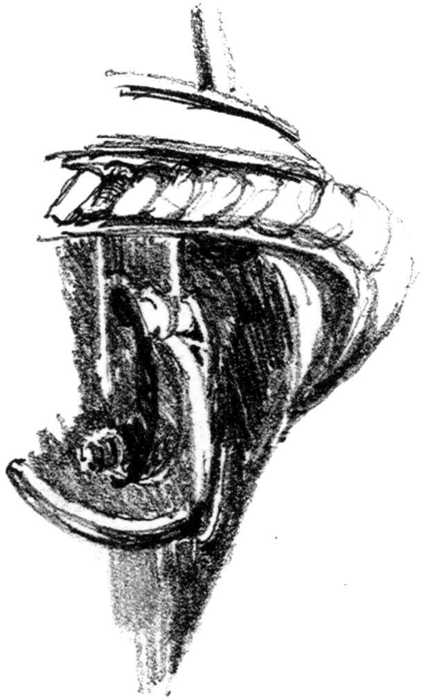

We encountered many of the classic sailing ships of old, now converted to passenger vessels plying the tourist trade – all had priority of place at moorings in the town centre.

Where could a private boat such as ours find space amongst the mass of yachts, barges, motor boats and dinghies all seeking access to the open water beyond?

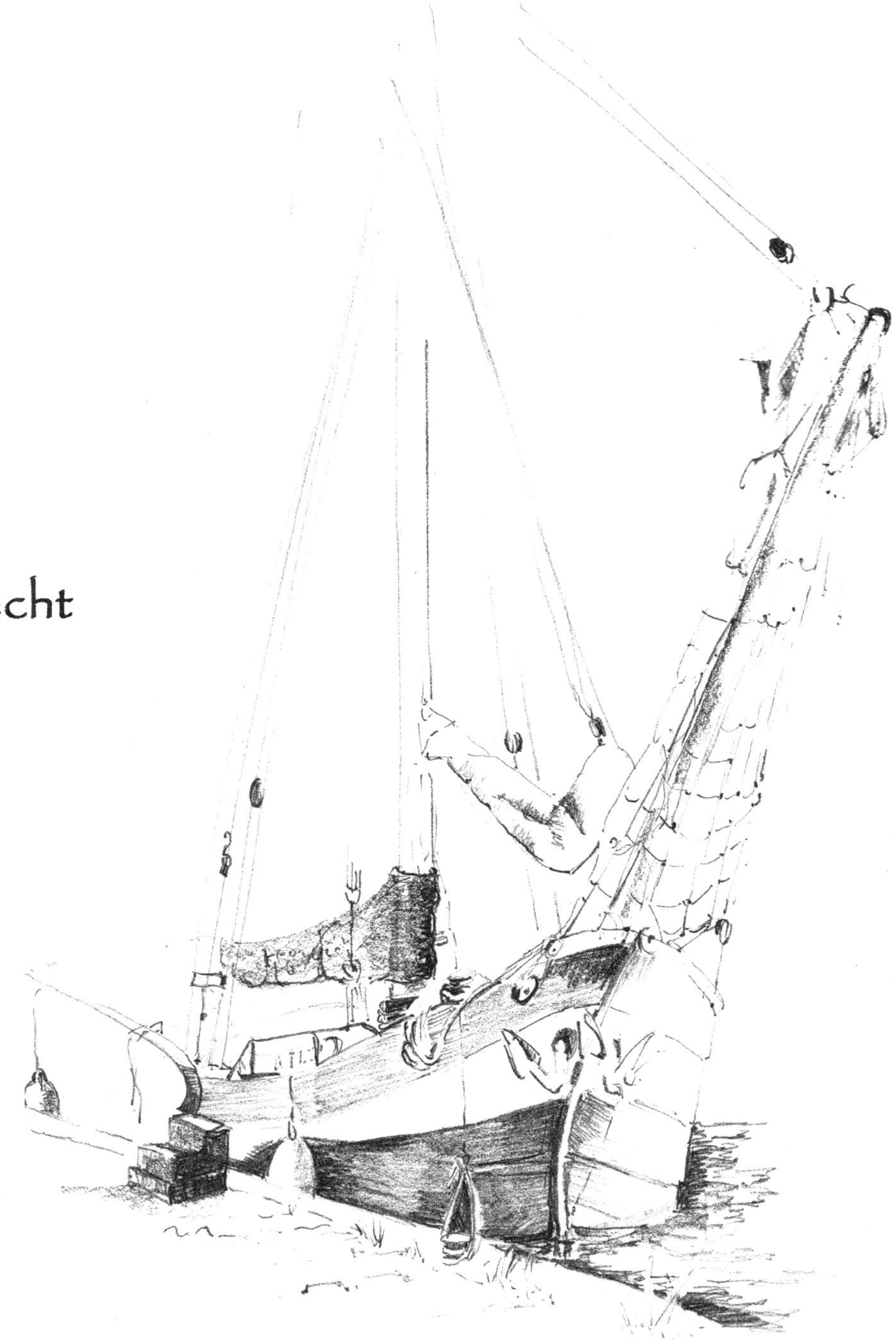

Continuing through the lock it is often possible to find space at the mouth of the river at one of the busy marinas from which one can walk back to explore the town. It is hard to imagine a more romantic view. We had been allotted an outer berth right opposite the grand old brick fortress of Muiderslot, built in 1204 to defend the entrance to the Vecht.

The River Vecht

A pencil image of Muiderslot was drawn in a few moments as we docked. Often there is not time to complete a sketch when passing by. I keep my paintbox on the cabin table, and between calls to help with nautical issues I may be able to refine a drawing or add a colour wash to the scene.

Our viewpoint was little changed. I worked on the drawing again when power was connected, water tank filled and dues paid, remembering the advice of a tutor once given: "don't ever guess – stop drawing when you can see no more!"

On another occasion we berthed on the East bank. The castle still dominated the scene.

A haunting memory of Muiden stays with us – a backdrop of the castle walls floodlit on a magic mid-summer evening whilst under a full moon the last yachts returned from the IJsselmeer, their rippling shadows drawn upon the darkened waters.

Overnight mooring in the marina at Naarden

Naarden

The history of the long wars against the Spaniards may be read elsewhere, but every port around the Zuiderzee had been fortified against the invaders and the remains of these fortifications has remained an influence on infrastructure to this day.. Naarden fell to the Spanish in 1572, but the stronghold remains, shaped as a 12 pointed star with no less than 6 bastions surrounded by a double ring of walls and canals. This cannot fail to impress and is well worth a visit.

Typical Friesland pasture

Our journey was to take us up to Friesland. We could either head straight north through the open waters of the Markermeer and the IJsselmeer or we could take a longer route enabling us to stop by at some of the old fishing ports, isolated from the open sea since the building (1927-1932) of the Afsluitdijk. Soon after the enormous project to enclose the waters of the former Zuiderzee was completed, three huge polders were created, which greatly increased the agricultural lands N.E. of Amsterdam. A further plan to create another, the Markerwaard polder, was abandoned, doubtless to the relief of the many sailors who today enjoy this stretch of open water so close to the city of Amsterdam.

The construction of the dike and enclosure of the waters of what then became the IJsselmeer, brought great benefits. Over 555,000 acres of fertile land was created, the danger of flooding was greatly decreased, and no longer was the salinity of the land increased by natural disasters. Sadly, however, many of the old ports declined as the fishing fleets could no longer find plentiful shoals nearby, and overseas trade was channelled through the major ports of Rotterdam and Amsterdam.

Kampen – at the mouth of the River IJssel

In the Middle Ages both Elburg and Kampen were prosperous trading and herring ports. Commercial routes extended to the Baltic. The fall in prosperity began in the C16 under the influence of Spanish occupation and with the gradual silting of the Zuiderzee. The decline of the fishing industry which followed the building of the Afsluitdijk led to Kampen reducing in importance to become a minor river port. Many historic buildings and monuments remain from the Golden Age, and a small display of both reconstructed and genuine old fishing and trading vessels can be seen in the restored old harbour.

A modern marina now lies beyond the old harbour with its historical craft, preserved for us all to enjoy.

Overijssel

From Kampen the choice of route to Friesland is full of options. The land of Overijssel is endowed with lakes and meers, linked by canals and streams. Much of what we see today was formed by the digging of peat from the bogs. The canals were cut in order to transport the turf. Many attractive farmhouses and pretty thatched cottages line the banks, the tended flowerbeds sweeping to the water's edge. Many have private landing stages or jetties set under shady willows where the owners' craft rock gently at their moorings.

A random route selected through this area is sure to please. Summer visitors may hire rowing boats, punts or canoes. But we are free to move on at will, pausing to watch the wildfowl dodging through the reeds, the fisherman setting his eel nets, the labourer gathering rushes for thatch or perhaps we may be lucky enough catch a glimpse of a shy otter searching for prey.

A night was spent in a quiet backwater of Blokzijl, formerly one of the prosperous ports much used by Dutch East Indiamen for shelter from winter storms. A dinner eaten at the Kaatje bij de Sluis is reward indeed after a few hours spent on deck with brush in hand!

Sneek and the surrounding lakes

The route north to Sneek can be varied according to one's need for draft. Much of the way will lead through quite large areas of lakeland which are deceptively shallow, but with well marked channels, often passing close to reed beds and lily pools – a treat for the observant naturalist and bird watcher.

At the centre of the fenland area that is so popular with summer tourists lies the town of Sneek, once a port on the Middelzee, an inland sea which has now disappeared. The imposing brick and sandstone Waterpoort (1613) then protected the town, its arched arcaded gateway forming a bridge over the Geeuw, a landmark recognised by all who visit during the popular summer season.

Students, pensioners, mothers with children, young and old alike, often rest awhile to enjoy the sight of boats in the pool by the Waterpoort.

Sneek, the Waterpoort

Sneek and the surrounding lakes

Sneekermeer and the nearby waters of Feanen are favourite areas for all kinds of waterborne activity. There were holidaymakers in rubber tyres and on surf boards, in canoes and dinghies, in every make and size of sail boat ever designed - both modern and traditional, in motor boats and cruisers big and small, and even aboard a paddle steamer of some size with red painted tines which seemed to have lost its way from the Mississippi!

Quick sketches of passing craft

Sneek and the surrounding lakes

It was 6.30 p.m. on a beautiful summer's evening – as if the school bell had rung, all the sailors headed home! We lay quietly at our mooring listening to the sounds of the birds and the wind in the reeds.

Coots are a comon sight on all Dutch waterways, always argumentative over territorial rights!

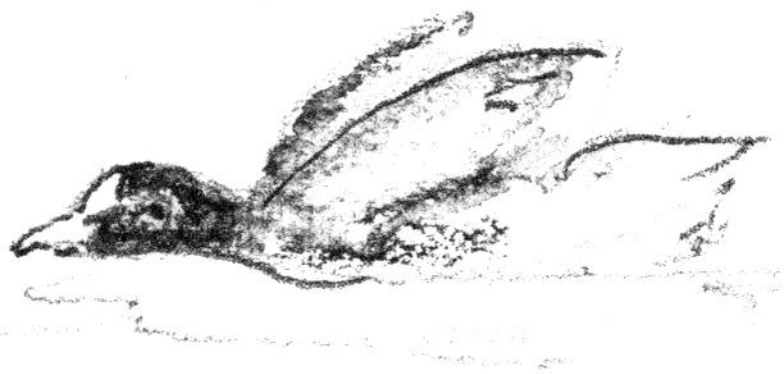

We rose with the larks. As the grey mists of dawn lifted slowly from the reed beds to melt softly into the early rays of weak sunshine a big flock of lapwing took off from the field of unmown hay that lay behind the bank where we were moored. No other craft were to be seen. Did we disturb fish that lay in peace below our hull as we began our day? For whatever reason we were overtaken time and time again by two pairs of cormorants who would land gracefully, feet extended, some 15 feet ahead of our bow, then dive, often to emerge minutes later with a fat fish held firmly n beak.

Cormorants were frequently sighted along the water channels.

Much of the waterway between the IJsselmeer and the centre of Friesland passes through privately owned farmland. Individual owners are permitted to charge "bruggeld" – a toll for the opening of the bridge. This is collected by an operator who, from the window of a kiosk, extends a simple fishing rod from the line of which dangles a clog. The clog is positioned over the cockpit of each and every passing craft. The crew must deftly catch the swinging clog and place the correct toll within – no stop is necessary.

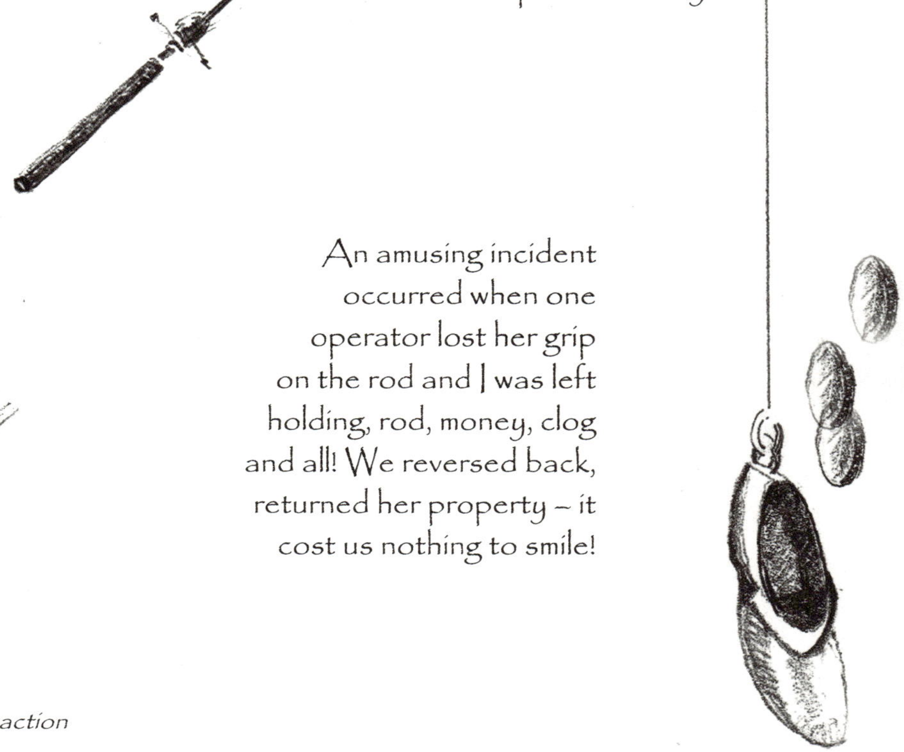

Leaving behind us the busy waterway town of Sneek, heading west, we stopped at a conveniently placed jetty set in the reed beds in order to visit the working mill at IJlst. This was a saw mill, working in the old way – seven or eight parallel blades powered by the wind moved to create planks from whole tree trunks. We learned that the miller was working to fulfil an order for a restoration project in Zaandam.

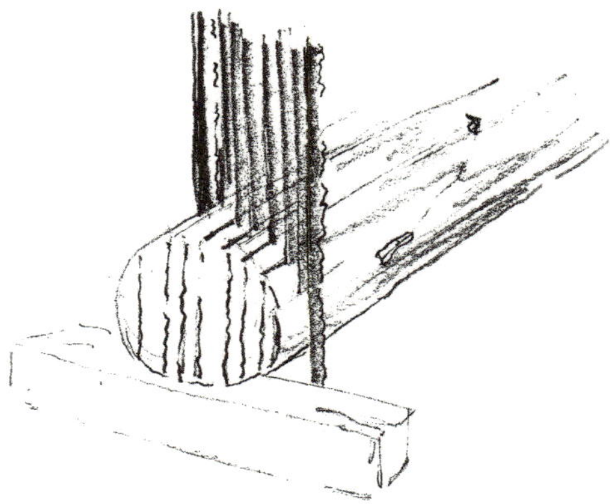

Sketch of the parallel blades in action

An amusing incident occurred when one operator lost her grip on the rod and I was left holding, rod, money, clog and all! We reversed back, returned her property – it cost us nothing to smile!

Friesland – IJsselmeer towns

Lemmer is a natural watersport centre, situated as it is, on one of the most direct routes from Amsterdam into the centre of Friesland. One lock leads into the open waters of the IJsselmeer.

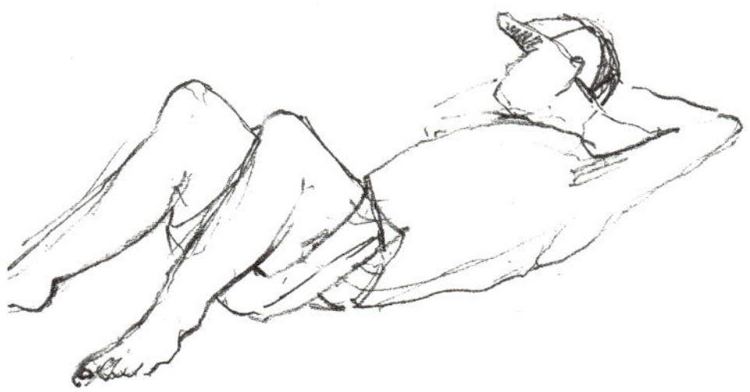

With sighs of relief we prepare to move on!

Before we dared venture out we had a problem to solve. As we left Sneek – we had felt a vibration through the steering wheel. The waters of Tjeukemeer, the largest lake in Friesland, are shallow, allowing no deviation from the marked channel. It seemed as if we had something around our keel. It was impossible to dive and check for an obstruction. Each cut we passed was silted and narrow, each lake we crossed was marked with a narrow buoyed channel. It was too shallow to anchor and too murky to see. No chance to dive. No casual floating plastic bag this, but something more serious.

Help!

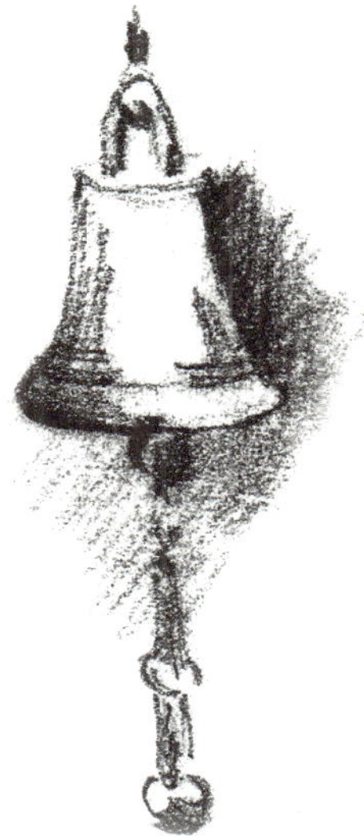

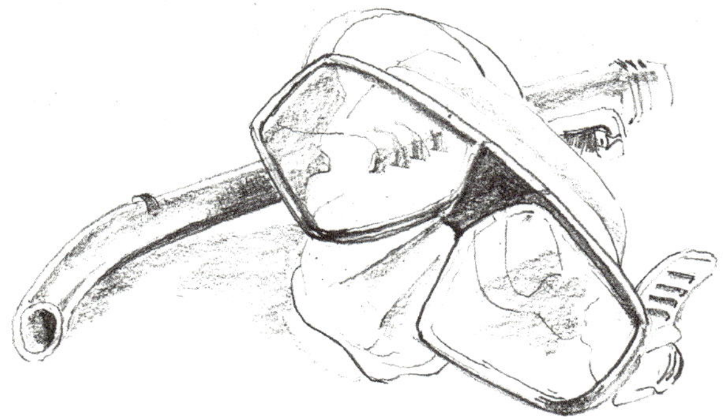

We limped slowly to Lemmer where we found a yard able and willing to lift the boat – there it was .... a bundle of washing, stockings and shirts, shredded plastic and cord, discarded or dropped by accident in the canal and now tightly wrapped around our propeller! All was cut free in minutes!

Hindeloopen – no way inland – the lock entrance is too narrow for a Linssen!

Friesland – IJsselmeer towns

Herring and eel are still caught from these ports, but since the building of the Afsluitdijk access to the North Sea is restricted, and the industry has declined steadily. Whilst waiting for the lock to open I sketched what may be one of the last remaining working vessels, seen here at Makkum.

Makkum – working fishing vessel

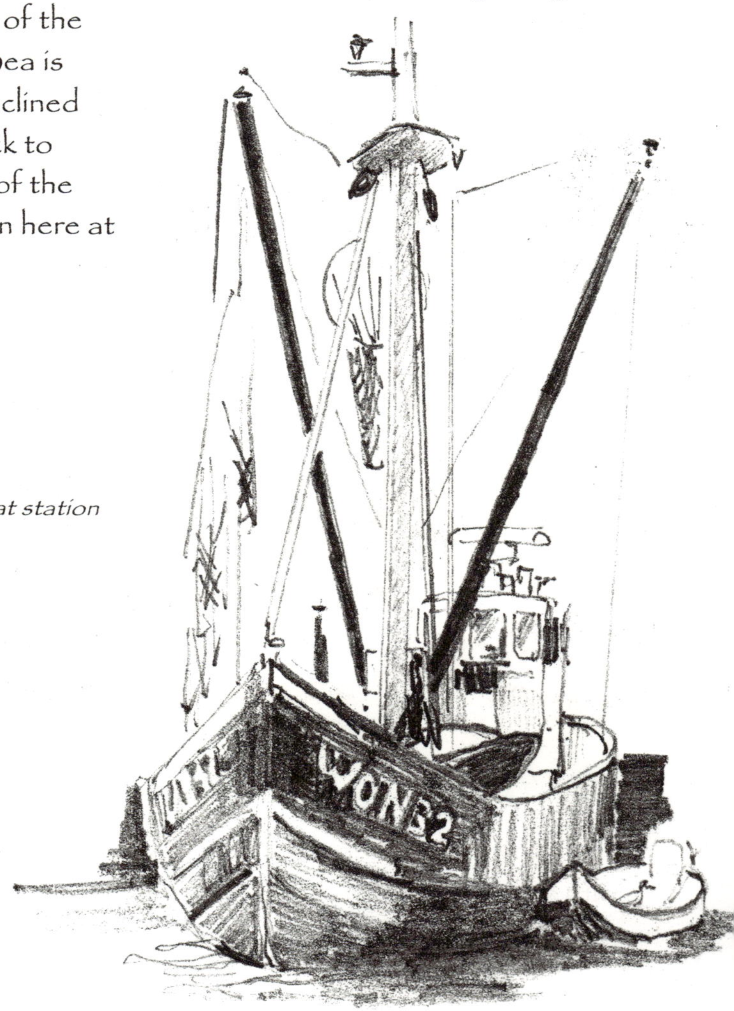

The old lifeboat station

Hindeloopen was a flourishing community in the 17th and 18th centuries when 200 or more boats sailed regularly to Scandinavia and Russia in search of trade. Today there are fewer than 800 residents, but the town is well known for the style of painted furniture that once was produced here. A unique house, dating back to 1619 lies beyond the narrow entrance to the lock. This is currently the home of a friendly harbourmaster.

Stavoren is the oldest city in Friesland, having been granted City rights back in 1118. Today with less than 1000 inhabitants however, the quiet town cannot compare with its rich and wealthy status in the early Middle Ages when vessels from this harbour sailed regularly north to Baltic ports and south to Spain, Portugal and beyond in search of trade, bringing back silks and jewels, artworks and silver as well as trade goods of many kinds.

Now this peaceful town offers summer visitors shelter in a secluded harbour with a ferry service to Enkhuizen. You may see a bronze statue of the Lady of Stavoren standing on the quayside. Her story is interesting.

Friesland – IJsselmeer towns

Legend of the Lady of Stavoren

The legend tells us the story of a sea captain who fell in love with an inhabitant of Stavoren, a rich and proud widow, who aimed to outdo all other merchant ladies, wearing the very best and most expensive of silks and jewels. Overlooking her greedy indulgent ways, this captain proposed to her and was accepted, on condition that he return with the richest treasure he could find. Many months later he came – to her horror bringing a full cargo of wheat, but no jewels. He claimed the wheat could feed many many hungry people – a great treasure indeed for without daily bread what use are all the treasures in the world? She, mortified and ridiculed by all, refused to accept the gift and told the captain to dump it in the sea. A beggar told her that if she were to waste the wheat she would become poor herself. In temper she threw a ruby ring into the harbour claiming the day the ring was found she would be poor. The ship sailed, and the captain jettisoned the entire cargo overboard just beyond the harbour. Some months later the sea receded, the seeds sprouted trapped in grains of sand and a golden harvest was reaped. But the bank upon which it grew prevented vessels from entering the harbour and the Golden Years were over - trade was no longer possible. After the captain had sailed, the Lady gave a banquet to prove she was still wealthy – at the banquet a fish was served – in its mouth was found the ruby ring!

To this day, there is a sandbar outside the harbour, named the Lady's Sand. Sailors beware!

Hoorn, the watchtower

IJsselmeer ports – the West coast

Hoorn, on the Western side of the IJsselmeer has a delightful inner harbour entered after passing a fleet of century old sailing barges moored beneath the Hoofdtoren or watchtower.

The Veermanskade quay is lined with fine restored merchants' houses, many of which have carved stones or friezes depicting marine features of the C16. Façades frequently sport tall narrow windows separated by carved wooden pilasters. It was from one such house that William Schouten became the first man to round the southernmost point of Tierra del Fuego in 1616. He was to name this Cape Horn after his native town.

Markermeer
Hoorn

This wily old heron used to sit daily on the structure of the bridge marking the entrance to an inner smaller canal within his beady eye alive to all that passed by and all that lay below.

With a Force 8 summer gale blowing out at sea it was little hardship to wait awhile in the delightful old inner port of Hoorn, surrounded by timeless well preserved Dutch merchant houses, each with its varied gabled or stepped roof. From a vantage point on the comfortable deck of our boat I was able to paint undisturbed by curious onlookers.

At the northern end of the quay was a delightful restaurant

C16 merchant houses on the quay, Hoorn

When the weather abated we headed for Enkhuizen, yet another of the IJsselmeer ports that have been in decline since the Golden Years and the end of commercial fishing. This latter, we know, was largely due to the silting up of the Zuiderzee, and the building of dams across the former shallow sea which prevented the free movement of fish stocks.

Drawbridge linking the Dromedaris (watchtower) with the City centre

Its strategic position as a key maritime city lost in history, the townsfolk of Enkhuizen now have to look to other means to sustain their livelihood. Tourism plays a big part in this, for the city centre holds some fine buildings, and links with the maritime past are continued through the building of new marinas and centres for water sports. An outdoor Museum flourishes which reflects village life throughout the past centuries. Many buildings of historical interest have been relocated here.

Time was moving on, and a busy schedule called for more rapid progress. Unable to buy a chart of the open sea beyond the Afsluitdijk, we dared to rely upon electronic navigation for the short leg of some 12 nautical miles to Den Helder.

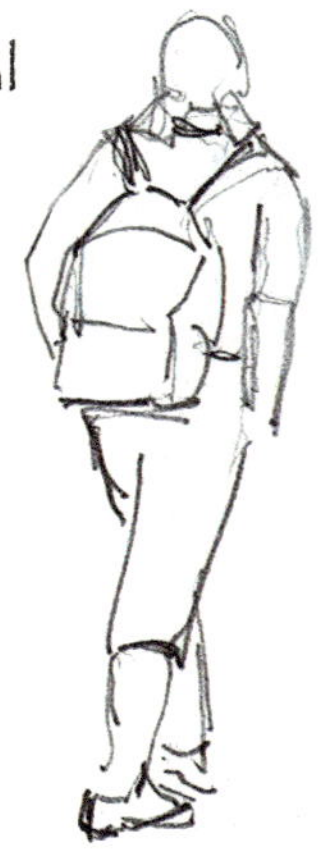

Our route would take us down the Noord-Hollands canal, and into Amsterdam, passing through mainly agricultural land. This canal was much in use before the building of the North Sea Canal leading directly from IJmuiiden to the City, but now carries little commercial traffic.

IJsselmeer to Den Helder

Modern wind farms today replace many of the polder mills that used to drain the land.

Noordhollands Kanaal - Alkmaar

Many long straight orderly stretches of this canal cut through farmland drained and apportioned by wealthy Amsterdam merchants searching for extra nearby land over 100 years ago. Today these boundaries still retain their mathematical and orderly precision.

The ancestors of the Amsterdam merchants were most unpopular with the local countryfolk for, placing profit before patriotism, they had provided supplies of food to the occupying Spanish army during the 80 Years War. It was only when heavy rain flooded the surrounding countryside that the 16,000 strong Spanish forces had been forced to withdraw.

It was late in the season. By mid October the spectacle of the weekly cheese market in Alkmaar was over. We made a brief stop by the magnificently housed harbour master's office, and joined the crowds of tourists in town.

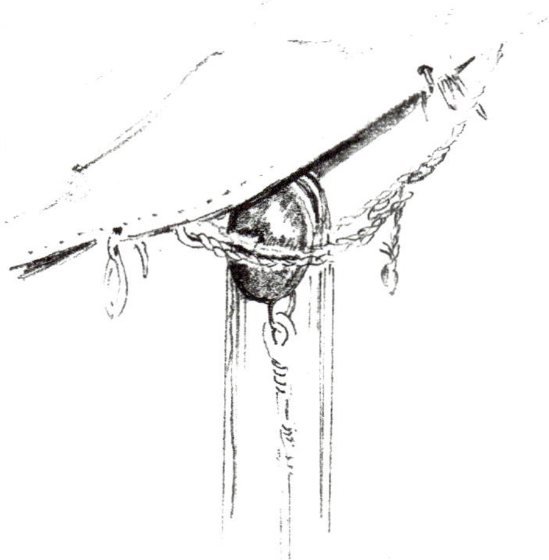

Adjusting the angle of inclination

Polder mills nearby were small and squat, many with thatched sides, frequently turning to drain water from the fields into well defined ditches and channels.

We had been out of touch with news and home for too long! It was time to stand our dish on the quay and search for the elusive satellite that would bring the world of news into our cabin. We hate to admit the truth, but this is a primitive method, and an expensive installation could ease the tension each time we try!

The southerly route chosen took us down through Wormerveer where we circled twice in order for me to make a quick sketch of an end of terrace home that been in the Dutch side of our family for many years. This brought back childhood memories to the skipper who had learned much of his watercraft on this stretch of water! To our surprise it had now become the office for a housing agent!

Zaanweg 7, Wormerveer

Nearing Amsterdam, we passed through the area of Zaanstreek. Today a historical collection of mills have been reconstructed and preserved in what may well have been one of the very earliest industrial regions in the world. As early as 1592 the first wind powered sawmill was built here and by 1760 as many as 600 mills were operating, variously used in the manufacture and processing of paper, oil, paint and tobacco.

It is not possible to view the best of Amsterdam from the water in a boat of our size. Plenty of tours of the narrow Amsterdam canals are available. Facilities for docking can be found at a central marina, but all expeditions are best conducted on foot.

The shipping forecast was bad – force 8 gales and heavy rain. This time we pressed on, exposed to the worst that nature can provide, amused to see clusters of ducks, feathers blown inside out, ruffled and disturbed, barely able to stand at the water's edge.

The route on to Aalsmeer lies through the western part of the City, unremarkable save for the number of bridges, both road and rail, for which one must await the opening.

The Zaan and Alsmeer

Orchids for auction

An early morning visit to the flower market was a revelation. 13 auction halls simultaneously hum with activity – all is now electronically controlled. An endless stream of trolleys passes by as details of each lot are flashed upon a huge screen. Buyers sit at tiered desks, each with a computer. 20 million cut flowers and 2 million plants are sold daily! Many will be aboard a plane at nearby Schiphol before the day is out.

The City walls of Gouda were largely removed 150 years ago, and further 'improvements' were made in 1940 when many canals were filled in. How fortunate that so many local people protested at the destruction of all these features so that we, today, may enjoy those that remain.

Gouda

The market town of Gouda brings to mind the cheese for which it is so well known. For those of us "in the slow lane" with time to spare there is so much more. A short diversion leads one into small canals where if fortune smiles it is possible to moor along the quay and walk to the city centre. The C15 Gothic City Hall stands tall and elegant, dominating the central square which is alive with custom on market days. This ancient town has suffered much throughout history, and economically has experienced its periods of power and wealth followed by depression and disasters – fire and plague both were responsible for bringing times of hardship. We moored in the old harbour opposite the Museum, and joined other visitors in the Grote St Jans Kerk (1530-1600), which even in the C17 attracted tourists who came to view the exceptional stained glass windows within.

We delayed too long and left in haste – the exit under the bridge spanning the lock looked all too low. The lock keeper looked seriously concerned. Could we clear the it? The water rose – the onlookers stared, secretly hoping for some dramatic action! We dropped all canvas in record time – 50 studs to release, split pins to remove and steel struts to lower – only 2 of us aboard. We made our exit, re-erecting the awning as soon as we reached the safety of a vacant pier. We had passed that way before, but in a smaller boat! Those afloat beware - always remember to check your air draft!

We were still far from our home base of Maasbracht. It was time to move south. Pressing on, we passed industrial areas near to the outskirts of Rotterdam, meeting many commercial barges hurrying to deliver cargo.

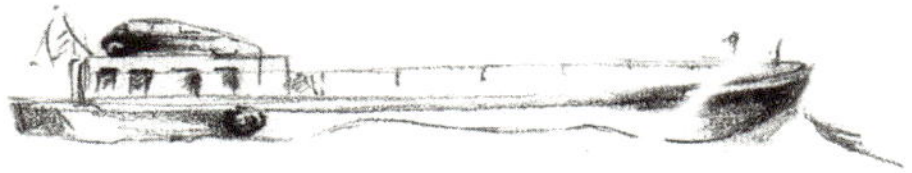

Dordrecht – Beneden Merwede

At last the long waterfront of Dordrecht appeared on our bow. Our charts advised that there were harbours right inside the old town. The entrance was hard to see. A small lift bridge was raised and we gained access to a delightful narrow inlet, the Vlijhaven, which was surrounded by a classic variety of gabled houses on either side. Before dusk fell we walked to absorb the atmosphere of this interesting town with its canals and quays, old façades, cobbled streets, narrow lanes, iron bridges and boats of all shapes and sizes.

It was a Sunday morning. As we left our mooring quietly passing out of our sheltered haven on to the fast flowing stretch of river, here known as the Beneden Merwede, we heard the 64 bells of Grote Kerk ring out. A last look back at the town showed the church tower rising high above the surrounding buildings, the four faces of the clock standing mysteriously aloft, bereft of surrounding masonry. We learned that the tower has remained unfinished since the year of 1502 because of subsidence then found on the northern side. Despite the techniques available to builders in later centuries the clocks stand alone as if awaiting the builders to awaken from their sleep to finish the job!

We battled upstream again the current, fast flowing following the heavy rains of autumn, all traces of the sandy beaches so popular in summer now hidden by broken water, the breakwaters marked only by radar reflectors mounted high on poles rising through the waves warning us to steer clear. The season was nearly over.

The cattle still grazed the water's edge, as did the sheep, their lambs now grown fat and healthy. The flocks of water birds seemed larger than before, young and old alike, bickering and fighting over some tasty morsel. Many would soon depart for winter feeding grounds.

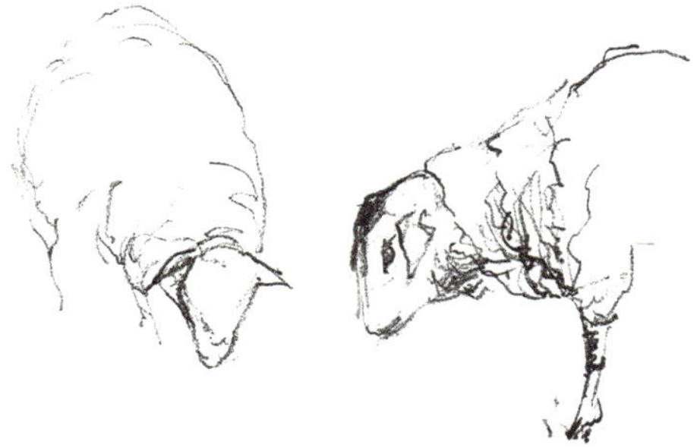

It was time for us to write the last log and prepare for the cold months ahead. The boat would be lifted from the water, prepared and stored until we were ready to use her again.

Continuing our hard won passage upstream, now grateful for shelter beneath our covered steering position on deck, wipers working to clear the never ending burst of rain, we noted the great numbers of cormorants resting atop the radar reflectors on our port side, the inverted triangular shape so convenient for a perch. Those to starboard were of course devoid of such facility having been designed without thought for avian comfort and convenience!

The Maas

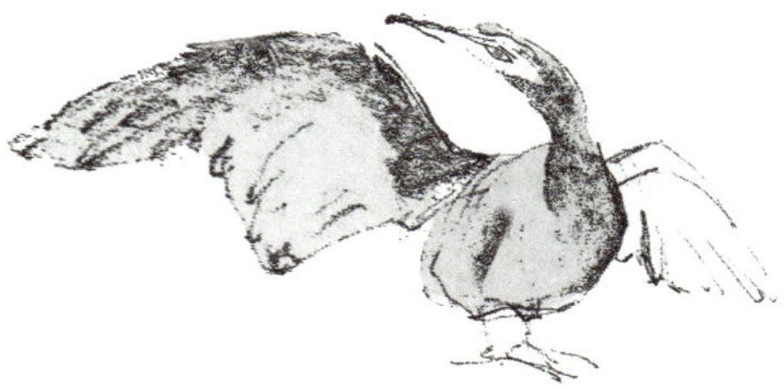

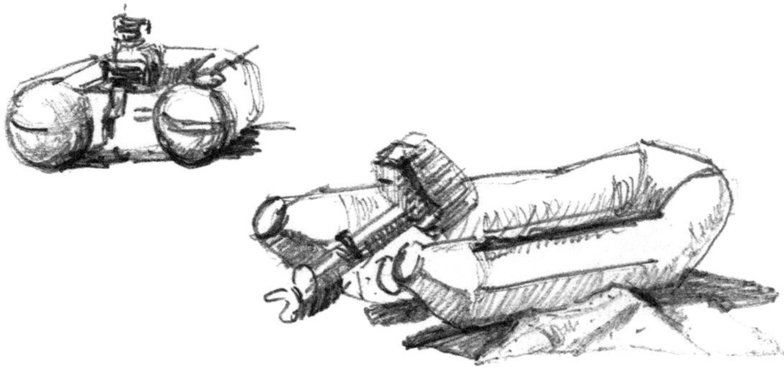

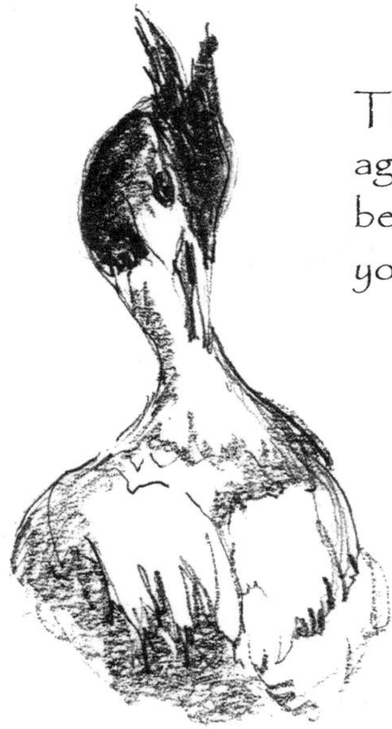

The cycle of life is renewed again as the ritual of courtship begins, nests are made and the young fledglings hatch.

Grebe : colourful courting display

Launching and recovery by hoist

Spring is here again, boats are taken out from winterstorage, launched, refuelled and prepared. Owners are busy making improvements, loading stores, checking dinghies and making all ready for the holidays ahead.

New owners begin to explore the delights of cruising and old hands return to discover anew the cruising pleasures enjoyed in previous seasons.

Perhaps this year we should turn south, cross the nearby border into neighbouring Belgium, and see how different this small country might be?

The Least Water Lily, floated freely in shallow water along the banks.

We chose to take the Zuid Willemsvaart Canal. To our surprise we found varied rural countryside – we could have been in France! There was little traffic to remind us of busy City life left behind. A kindly lock keeper extended a hook to take our warps up the long green and slippery 8 metre wall. The waters rose – we completed forms to permit us to travel the Belgian waterways and continued our way.

Despite the peaceful scene of grazing cattle, fields of growing corn and the chatter of families of fledgling birds, we were reminded of the time when this area was of strategic importance during the last war. Derelict pill boxes, still bearing the scars of gunfire, lay at intervals along the eastern bank, built, we learned, by Belgian conscripts under German orders during the occupation. Bocholt, the border crossing, lay where road, rail and river meet, and was an important centre for distribution of supplies, vulnerable and heavily guarded.

One of the many pill boxes that remain still showing the scars of war.

Rekum - just one tower of the castle is visible from the water

Zuid Willemsvaart canal

An avenue of old lime trees to one side of a cobbled street struggled to maintain a tenuous hold on life. Some bore hollowed trunks – one we noticed had been filled in a whimsical way with supporting brick into which was set a tiny door – the creator perhaps a childhood reader of Winnie the Pooh, and inspired by A.A. Milne, remembered piglet's house as he played out his fantasy?

Rekum canalside home

A pleasant overnight mooring was found at the little village of Rekem, dominated by an impressive castle. We could only catch a glimpse of this above the trees!

3 fallow deer grazed under the apple trees in a small canalside garden, whilst a family of rats were seen to appear from a woodpile to feast upon the corn offered to the lone family hen!

Maastricht

Under a willow tree!

A glance at a botanical reference work aboard showed a surprising fact – no less than 25 different varieties of willow were listed. Perhaps we all remember that the wood was used in the manufacture of cricket bats? We learned that the bark of Goat Willow (pussy willow) is rich in tannin and is used in the curing of leather, and it also contains salicine – a substitute for quinine! The Chinese believe that the willow catkin is a symbol of new birth. It is chosen at the time of their New Year to bring good fortune into their homes.

Shortly the canal would divide – we could re-enter Holland and visit the historic town of Maastricht, or continue to join the Albert Canal, completed in 1846, to link the port of Antwerp with the industries around Liege.

In 2001 the inner basin in Maastricht was converted to a pleasant leisure area where crew may rest awhile and enjoy the convenience of attractive nearby restaurants and bars.

Wishing to head south, we had no choice but to follow the busy Albert canal upstream to Liege. The River Maas, now named Meuse, changes from the rural waterway beloved by all who sail the waterways of Holland, to a busy, wide and industrialised canalised section. Barges laden with coal, building materials and metals speed their way. Antwerp lies but 18 hours away for them. Even on this ubiquitous waterway, the watchful heron stands guard!

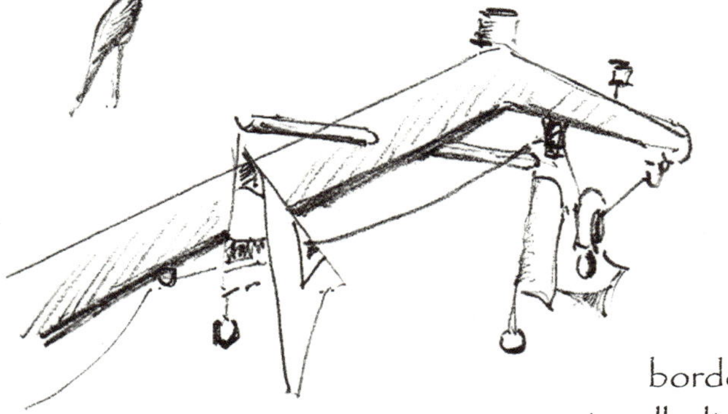

Masts lowered, but house flags and courtesy pennants still fly, weighted, correctly from some passing barges.

Commercial traffic delayed by the lock south of Liege

Belgium : La Meuse

How sharp the contrast when the border is crossed! High craggy cliffs occasionally lie to one side or the other. Soon the green fields of Holland give way to rising contours, tree lined slopes, different types of housing, churches and infrastructure. Pollution increases as varying factories discharge their effluent into air or water. Steel, glass, recycling, chemical production, building materials – all industries are served by the delivery of raw material, and the onward movement of finished product, by road, rail and of course by water.

Belgium industries line the banks

Fumes spew from the nuclear chimneys at Tihange

La Meuse - Liege

It was with relief that we at last left industrial surroundings and with interest that we entered the city of Liege and found safe mooring in a marina well placed to view the heart of this historic town. Although invaded and occupied many times, and damaged severely during the wars, new buildings have risen amongst the old, prosperity has returned, the University is flourishing and tourism is growing.

Tower of the Perron

We strolled from the central marina into the old part of town, viewed the magnificent Palais de Justice, the brilliantly coloured Hotel de Ville, and the Perron – a classified ancient monument, formerly the symbol of justice of the ruling prince bishops – now adopted as the symbol of the city. Cafes were full of happy tourists, and good business was done by all.

Sitting in the cockpit on a warm early summer evening I took the opportunity to sketch a fellow traveller, also southward bound.

We continued south – but time was short and we soon had to turn around. It was still early in the year. Our first short cruise of the season had to end. We will continue our exploration of the Dutch canals before long.

There is always activity in a busy shipyard – boats must be slipped for repair, and the wives of barge owners may need to go shopping or to visit home! This is one way to get the car out of the garage!

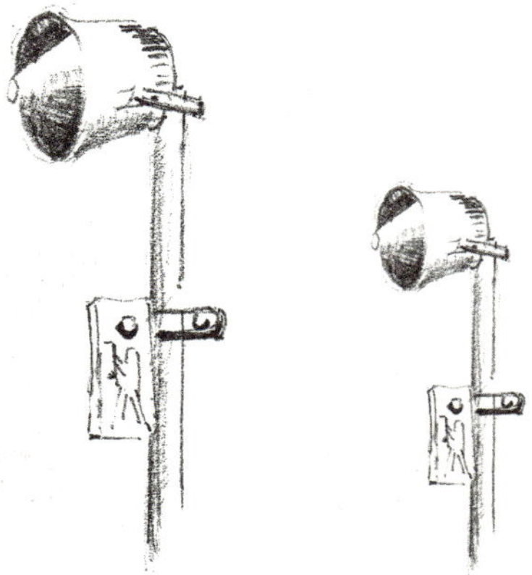

Dockside communication

Hauled out for a quick overnight repair.

A barge converted for private use lies in a side canal at 's Hertogenbosch.

A neglected dinghy lies beside a working tug in Maasbracht.

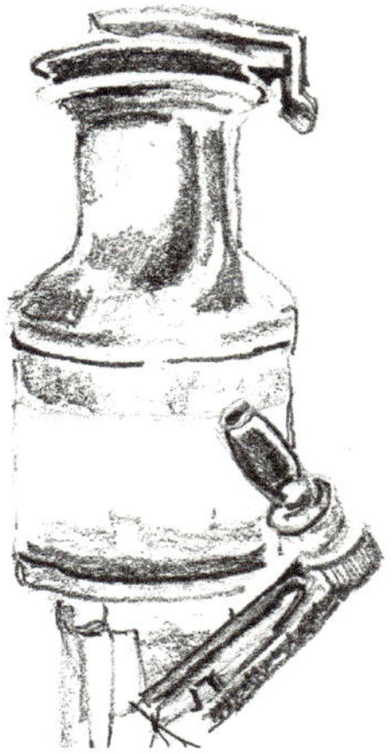

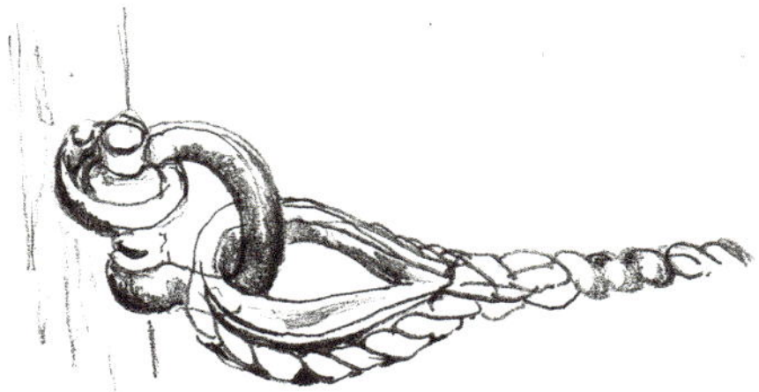

A walk around waterside facilities in many a marina near the main commercial routes will reveal a great diversity of craft.

We even noted a traditional English narrow boat in Maasbracht!

Grandchildren afloat!

Inactivity when grandfather is at the helm is so boo...oo..ooring!
We devise games to pass the time as we motor downstream.

"When are we going to stop for lunch?"
"When can we use the dinghy?"
"When can I have a turn?"
Children never change!

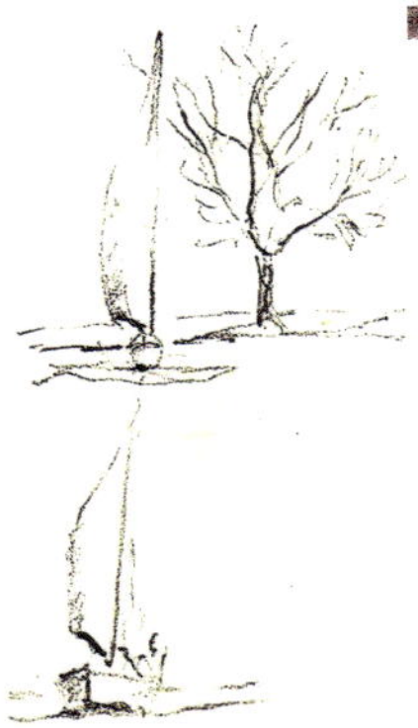

We note many trees along the banks of the Maas have been uprooted in recent strong winds.

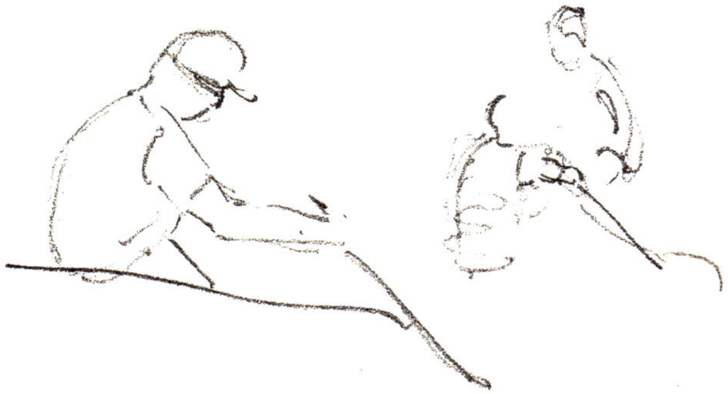

Learning new skills!

Young helmsman

We had been joined by two of our grandsons and their father for a few days. It is hard to keep active children interested and occupied when distance must be covered! We made frequent halts to lower the dinghy so that they could take turns in learning to handle the oars. Later promotion would give them a chance to handle it under motor – with father aboard to guard against any possible mishap.

"Where have they gone now?"

"Watch it – those swans can get nasty and cross!"

"Ducks are SO hard to draw because they won't sit still"

(Just like us!)

"Granny, please show us how."

"I will try but I don't find them easy to draw either!"

Meanwhile, father just has to find out what happens at the end of the last newly released Harry Potter!

No, the boys did not tell him the ending!

Oh dear!

Something went wrong! Father ordered ten minutes in detention!

Time out!

"If moving ducks are too difficult then we could try and draw things on the cabin table, boys."

A happy hour was spent as the two boys concentrated really hard on making a pencil study of the wooden fruit bowl. Above is Patrick's picture – at eight years of age he did well to observe carefully even if the lines don't always go where he wants! Jamie (eleven), had a more mature approach and showed a real understanding of form.

Dordrecht

This was our second visit to the town of Dordrecht .
This time we entered by way of the Nieuwe Haven, and lay on the western bank from which we had a splendid view of the Grote Kerk. The family returned home and we became tourists once more. An evening organ concert in the Grote Kerk made for a welcome cultural entertainment.

We learned an amusing tale – in the C17 a heavy tax was imposed on the import of cattle or sheep into the town. Two men intent on the age old game of tax evasion, dressed a sheep up as a man and attempted to pass by the authorities. All went well until the sheep said "baaa... baaa" and gave the game away!

Originally it was planned for the tower to rise to the height of 123 m. Subsidence, as we have told, prevented further building above the four clock faces. At 75 m the tower still dominates the moorings at the Nieuwe Haven. It houses what is said to be the largest carillon in Europe - 64 bells that ring cheerfully each and every 15 minutes of the day.

Hollands Diep

Willemstad

We had long been planning to visit this well restored fortified town on the edge of the Delta – the region where three big rivers, the Maas, the Rhine and the Scheldt break and divide, their channels ever changing throughout history and forming new islands, both due to natural circumstances and to the influence of man. Much of Holland lies below sea level, and has been flooded many times, always causing tragic loss of life. Following the latest major disaster in 1953 when flood waters reached inland as far as Dordrecht, Parliament resolved to close off all outlets to the North Sea (apart from the Westerschelde which leads to the busy port of Antwerp) and to build four massive dams across open water, the gates of which could be opened to allow a controlled tidal inflow. The full story of this massive engineering project is worth a study, but it is not for me to tell.

Detail of the traditional shuttering on the former town hall.

The harbour was crowded at the time of our visit with yachts gathering together for a one day regatta, perhaps the last of a series. The organisation of this event was conducted from the deck of 'Hendrika", moored on the quayside just astern of us. Happy celebrations continued for much of the night!

This splendid building, the former town hall, built in the C17, stands near to the quayside at the end of which is the d'Orangemolen, a tall brick built stage mill which dates back to 1734. Of great strategic importance at many times throughout its history, Willemstad was heavily fortified in the Middle Ages. The Arsenal dominates the western end of the old harbour. In 1944 the Germans again fortified the town as part of their Atlantic Wall strategy.

The racing fleet left and we could see once more from our deck the old flour mill that stands at the end of the Willemstad quay.

The window of this little house by the quayside in Zierikzee is so typical of many Dutch homes, evidence of the long maritime interest and involvement with the sea.

I caught a fleeting glimpse of a Willemstad bridal party before they moved off with a mounted guard of attendant to receive their friends.

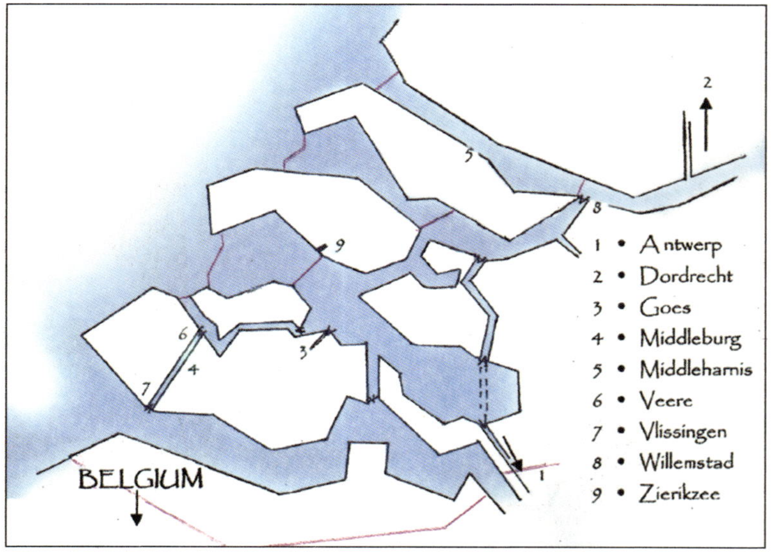

Days are so full and interesting when one is afloat, maybe resting in some newly discovered haunt, but now it was time to research ways by which we might explore the attractions of Zeeland.

Zierikzee - Zeeland

We experienced a big change as we left Willemstad and passed through the first lock on our way to Zierikzee. The sea breezes blew strongly over the stretches of open water that led to the Oosterschelde. Sea birds took the place of coots and ducks. Motor yachts were rarely seen – in their place sailing boats of modern design enjoyed the fine weather and free winds. The skies darkened as we made our way up the channel leading to the port of Zierikzee. We lay below the Zuidhavenpoort – an imposing gateway dating back to the C14 featuring four corner turrets. A fact remembered by schoolchildren is that in 1576 Spanish forces waded in shoulder deep water across from the mainland to capture the town.

Rows of elegant C17 and C18 houses, many restored after the great flood of 1953, line the quayside of the old harbour which is now reserved as a museum for historical vessels,. The boat I chose to draw was an old shrimping vessel, a Hoogars,, which would have had a bowsprit, built in 1878. She then had a skipper, 3 hands and a boy, and is still occasionally used today. Much of an extension to the Oude Haven was filled in in the C19. Today this area has become the pleasant centre of Havenplein, filled with cafés and bars, customers relaxing in historic surroundings with a well tended park nearby.

After experiencing rough weather and uncomfortable seas in an abortive attempt to visit the workings of the storm barrier, we sought shelter in the old town of Goes, reached by locking up into a stretch of canal 1 metre or so above sea level. We were allocated a berth in the 'binnenhaven' surrounded by delightful old houses.

Goes – Suid Beveland – Zeeland

It was market day – stalls selling local produce, materials, clothing, garden produce, haberdashery and trinkets filled the square, overlooked by the C15 stadhuis and the Grote Kerk, altered and much restored after the great fire of 1619.

Having replenished stores, we sat to enjoy a coffee before rejoining the boat, amused by the café customer sitting at the next table whose mouth was carefully wiped after every morsel of biscuit provided by his attendant owners.

Impeccably mannered, he waited, whilst they paid his bill, wagged his tail and was off!

And it was time for us to move on, too, this time after motoring past the flourishing mussel beds for which the region is so famous, we entered a further lock that took us into the fresh waters of Veersemeer – a popular holiday area for campers and yachtsmen alike. It was unfortunate that dull and stormy weather rather marred our approach to the delightful haven of Veere. We lay beneath the Campveerse Toren, part of the former fortifications, today, as it has been for the past 500 years, a tavern!

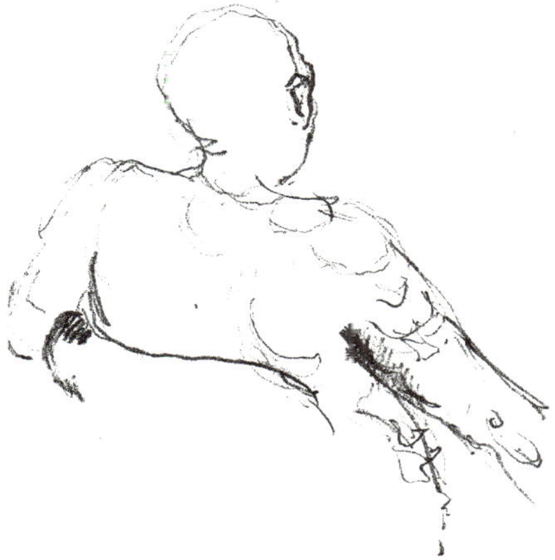

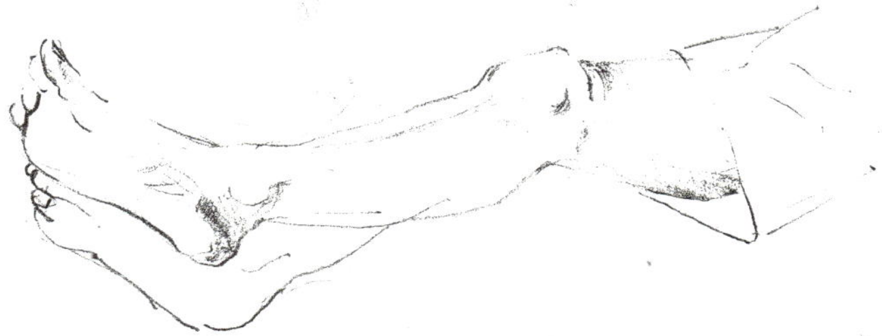

Different types of boat
and
different types of
sun worshippers!

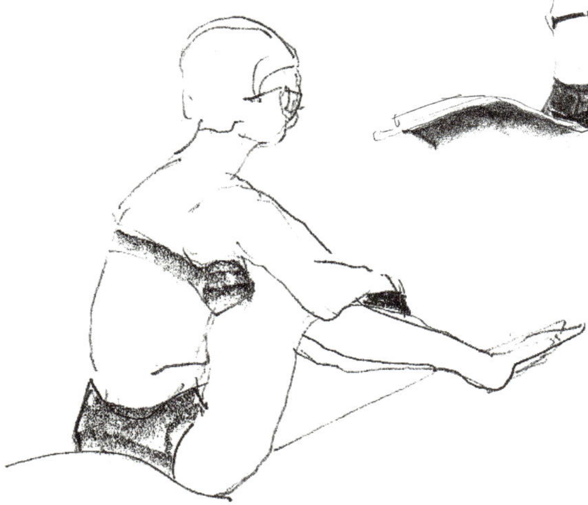

Veere - Walcheren

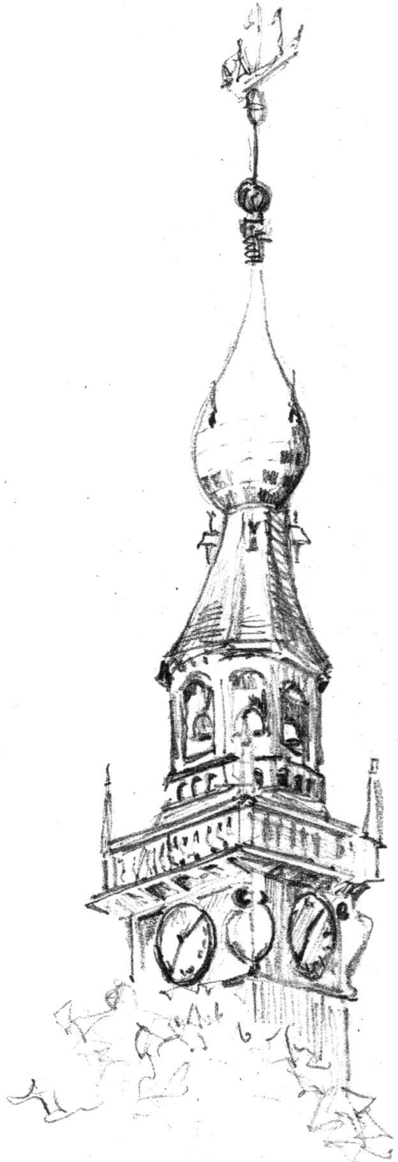

Veere was a prosperous port until construction of the storm barrier dams closed its access to the sea. It was a trading centre for Scottish wool between 1541 and 1799. Two enterprising Scottish merchants then established a monopoly for the sale of all wool into the Netherlands. Each Scot built in flamboyant Gothic style a remarkable house on the quay. No.25 which displays a weathered stone plaque featuring a lamb, symbol of the trade, is today a museum worthy of a visit.

Statues from the face of theStadhuis featuring noble men and women of the past were removed during renovations and replaced with replicas in the old style. The originals may be seen in the museum, safe from the vagaries of weather.

In the corner of one room, a kitchen, complete with copper kettle and pans, had been re-created. The alcove wall was lined with charming original old blue Delft tiles.

Viewed from the aft deck of our boat before stepping ashore for dinner was the impressive onion shaped belfry (1599) built over the sandstone Stadhuis (1474) which sounded a varied musical carillon of 48 bells every 15 minutes.

Middelburg Zeeland

The bustling town of Middelburg was our next port of call. An ornate geared wheel lift system raised the bridge so that we could enter the inner canal where we lay alongside the Rouaansekaai – used in times past to unload large cargoes of French wine shipped north from Rouen. Although heavily bombed during the last war, much of the City has been restored and rebuilt in its former style.

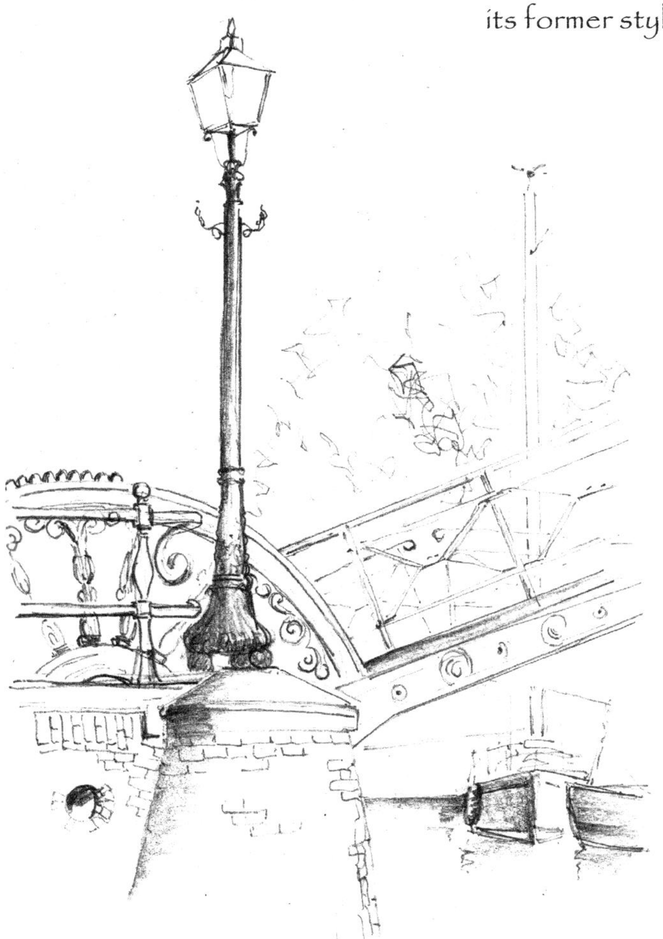

Warehouses line the end of Lordenskaai, some converted to become restaurants and bars. Our stay in Middelburg was to be short but we enjoyed a meal in this historical building – the street a memorial to the prosperous times when trade in cloth and wine brought great wealth to the town.

Approaching the Zeelandbrug

Calling again into Zierikzee, a stroll along the quay led us to observe the fishing boats returning with their catch of fresh mussels scraped from the beds which line much of the shore of the Oosterschelde.

Mussel net

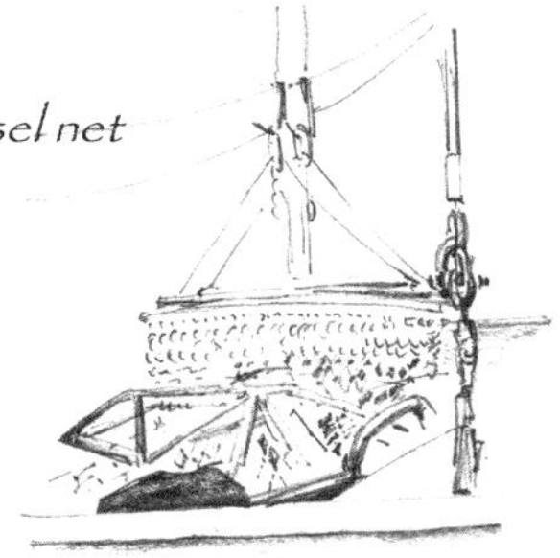

Mussel fishing boat, Zierikzee

Middelharnis - Delft

It was blowing Gale Warning Force 7 as we prepared to leave the Delta. Temporary shelter was enjoyed as we made slow progress through the lock back into the Hollands Diep. After spending a night in the calm of Middelharnis we worked our way through the busy harbour of Rotterdam. No place for sport boats here! We intended to move straight on to Delft, there to explore the charm of the old town with its shaded lime tree lined canals crossed by many picturesque humpbacked bridges.

It was hard to believe that the town was once considered to be a port of greater importance than Rotterdam. The height of town prosperity came as early as the C13 and C14, with trade being based upon the cloth and brewing industries. The water was so polluted then that even children drank beer – at one time there were 900 breweries in the area! Today the view of town seen from the moorings, bears little resemblance to the famous View of Delft immortalised by its famous resident, the artist Vermeer. Sadly, not one of his paintings remains in this his birthplace.

The Oostpoort – a fine view seen on passage through the main canal – slender turrets date from the C15 and C16.

In the late C17 the ceramic industry began in Delft. Today this is known worldwide for the production of "Delft Blue" – greatly influenced by the C18 import of china from the Orient, with relatively expensive items sold to the many tourists fortunate enough to visit the one remaining factory, that of Royal Delft. Master painters undergo many years of training to maintain the high standards of hand painted porcelain as produced in former years. Reproduction transfer tiles are also popular.

Master painter at work, Royal Delft

Sketchbook scribbles in the Kaag

We came across another Linssen – the 380 Sedan - it could be a perfect choice for two alone on the inland waterways.

Crossing through the chain of lakes forming Kaagerplassen we saw once more an abundance of wild life – cormorants atop the bare still sails of silent mills, swans gliding gracefully amongst the reeds, occasionally breaking into flight to land anew not far away, and the ever present noisy coots bustling about their business chasing all who presume to venture close.

The Kaag

Our days when possibly there was need to climb a mast to check a problem are long gone- now we can enjoy life the easier way – "in the slow lane"!

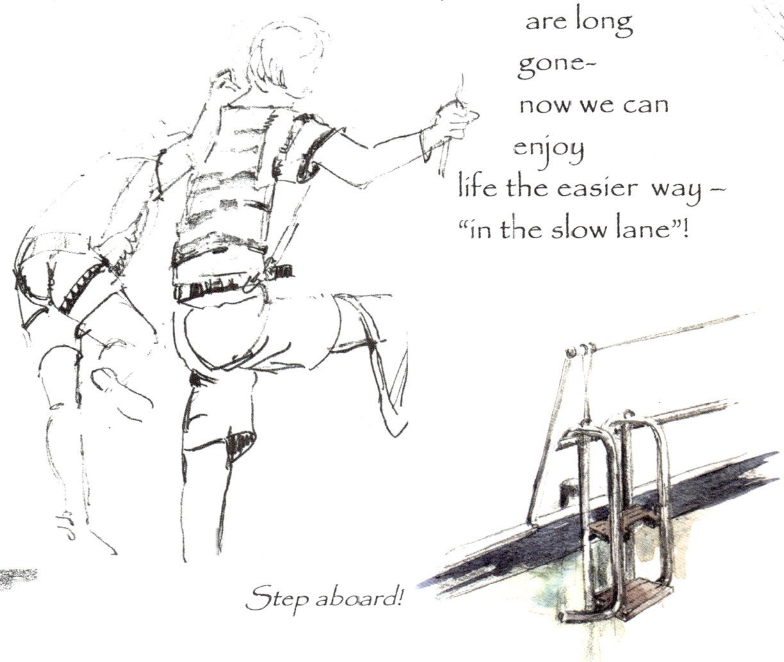

Step aboard!

With friends aboard we returned again to the town of Gouda. It was market day, the square beneath the architectural splendour of the mid C15 Gothic town hall was filled with colourful stalls. We lay within the town a short while to buy provisions.

Gouda canalside

Little time to stop for we had far to go ... it was time to move on again.

On an earlier page we described how, by leaving the Maas at Cuijk one could travel north to Germany, Friesland and beyond. It was time for us to head this way. Passage through the Maas-Waal canal was uneventful. We turned upstream and shortly came to Nijmegen. Moorings for short stay were available close to the famous Nijmegen bridge.

Nijmegen bridge as seen from the 'passantenhaven'.

Nijmegen is said to be the oldest city in Holland. The Romans, realising the strategic position of a base situated upon the hills overlooking the Rhine valley, built Noviomagus here.Many important archaeological finds have been made.

But it is the more recent history which many of us will recall. In 1944 a great number of citizens were killed when American air force planes mistakenly bombed the city, thinking it to be a German target. Much of the city centre was then destroyed.

Later in that same year it was of strategic importance for the Allied plan (code named "Market Garden"), in which hundreds of Allied troops were to be dropped by parachute in order to secure the bridge and allow the British Army to make what proved to be the tragic failure of the advance to Arnhem. The cost to human life was again very heavy.

Today Nijmegen is a thriving market town. A climb up to the Waag – in the central market square, is to be recommended. The waterfront is a bustling area in summer where pleasure boats frequently stop to allow tourists to view the surrounding river scene.

The Waal Nijmegen

By evening fishermen were jostling for space along an exposed sand bar.

Nijmegen – party time

We lay quietly at our mooring enjoying a glass of wine with good friends when new boats arrived. It was party time! Unaware of my interest they enjoyed the comradeship that comes after a day on the water.

As this is primarily a book about sketching – the impressions and emotions one can feel which are more personally felt, and remembered, when time is taken to commit pen and brush to paper, I thought it might be of interest to show how one such sketch was developed.

Time was, for once, on my side! My subjects were engrossed and unaware. I spent 10-15 minutes on sketching the scene which lay below us, then stopped to record the progress. Paintbox found, it then took only 10 minutes to complete a coloured impression of the scene. More memorable than a photograph – taken quickly, printed, stored and forgotten . By then it was time for a well earned dinner!

Waal to IJssel

We woke to find a thick fog enveloping our surrounds. River traffic continued without a break for the call of commerce is ever heard. We had no need to venture out - our plan was to visit the most northerly area of Holland. When we did leave our mooring we envied the ease with which the powerful barges motored up the Waal (Rhine). We held close to the banks keeping clear of the main currents and were pleased to find shelter at a marina close to the border. A visit to Arnhem could wait another day.

Refueling on the Rhine

Before it was our turn to refuel we noted the ingenious way in which this bunker station on the Rhine handled the problem for barge traffic. Our needs were attended to in more conventional manner!

We left the Rhine and joined the Ijssel, heading north downstream. Somewhat featureless this river nevertheless affords some interesting towns along the way. A halt was called at Doesberg where in a harbour filled with fibreglass boats of functional design, one classic craft caught my attention.

Yachthaven Bijland

The IJssel

Fast progress was made downstream heading for the historic fortress town of Zutphen. Flat farming country lay on both sides. Bird life was plentiful and we noted crested, little and grey herons, together with a few storks, and of course the ubiquitous flocks of pink footed chattering geese.

From our berth in Zutphen we had a splendid view of Sint Walburgiskerk which dominates this town of many towers. Altered throughout the intervening centuries, parts of this remarkable building date back to the C12.

Oarsmen were out in force – an annual racing event was taking place as we wound our way through their numbers taking care not to upset the light craft with our wash as we approached Zwolle.

The IJssel Zwolle

Facilities for waterborne visitors are ideal here. The old fortress city of Zwolle retains much of its former star shaped bastion layout. Moorings are conveniently placed along several of these walls. We were amused to watch our neighbours relaxing on the next boat, unaware that their contented mood was being recorded.

Neolithic remains have been found nearby. Zwolle is situated on a small rise between four rivers that proved to be safe from the flooding that reoccurred throughout the centuries. Much of the town within the walls has been preserved, and all becomes alive with activity on busy market days. We dined in candlelit surroundings in what had been for centuries the home of the public executioner!

At times most of us on the water experience one problem or another. We were no exception, and when a technical problem arose an enforced stop at the nearby Yachthaven Dijkzicht enabled me to record the contrasting scene – a 100 year old German estuary herring fishing craft set against the background of the very modern bridge over the Ijssel.

Waiting for a lift bridge to be opened

Noord-Willemskanaal

Heading north we chose to follow the Noord-Willemskanaal to Groningen – a route little used by commercial barges. The disadvantage of this was that lock-keepers and lift bridge operators were not keen to operate for one passing 'sport boat'. Delays became long and tedious whilst we waited for other boats to join us in each queue.

Every cloud is said to have its silver lining – there was more time to sketch or draw.

It was with with interest that we entered Groningen, the largest City in the north of Holland. Now we had joined the 'fixed mast' route which enables yachts of all sizes to proceed from the German and Baltic ports through to the North Sea without dropping their rigging. Bridges are either high enough to allow passage, or can be swung open for a brief period for river traffic. Groningen is a convenient stopover, and craft are well provided for in marinas right in the centre of this old town.
It was the start of a new University term, and the cafés were full of happy students renewing friendships .

We had to wait for the lock-keeper to finish lunch before we could proceed to the centre of town!

Holland has always been known as a country full of cyclists, but never had we seen so many as here! Shops abound with offers to sell, rent or repair bicycles of any make or age. Trade was busy!

Groningen

It was market day – the square was filled with stalls selling all manner of local produce. A high viewpoint was found from which I could admire the splendid façade of Martinikerk with the townsfolk below going about their business.

The tower – at 127 metres tall – was too high to fit on my page! The oldest part of the church (the transept crossing and 2 vaults within the nave), we learned, dates back to the C13.

But people lived here long before that date. Signs have been found of habitation which have been dated to nearly 4,000 years BC.

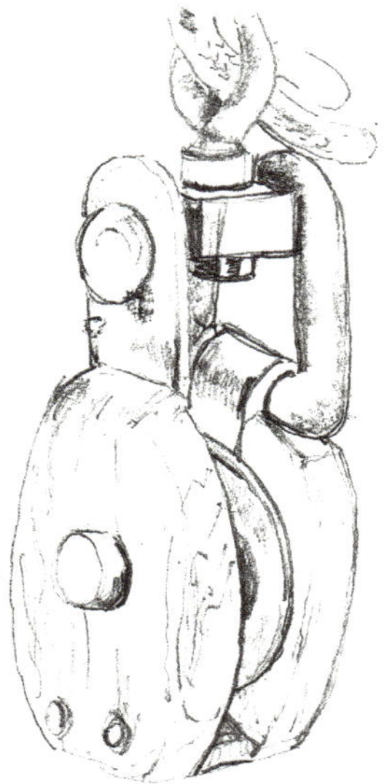

Groningen

Laden with purchases of fresh spinach, garlic, raspberries and cream and farmer's cheese, we returned to prepare dinner aboard and speak with interesting fellow travelers – all of whom have tales to tell.

Martinikerk, Groningen

It was time again to move on. We wished to see the most northerly point of Holland. We moved fast along the Eemskanaal with no locks to slow our progress or bridges that must be opened – for this was the 'fixed mast route' which led the way to the islands and the North Sea.

North Friesland

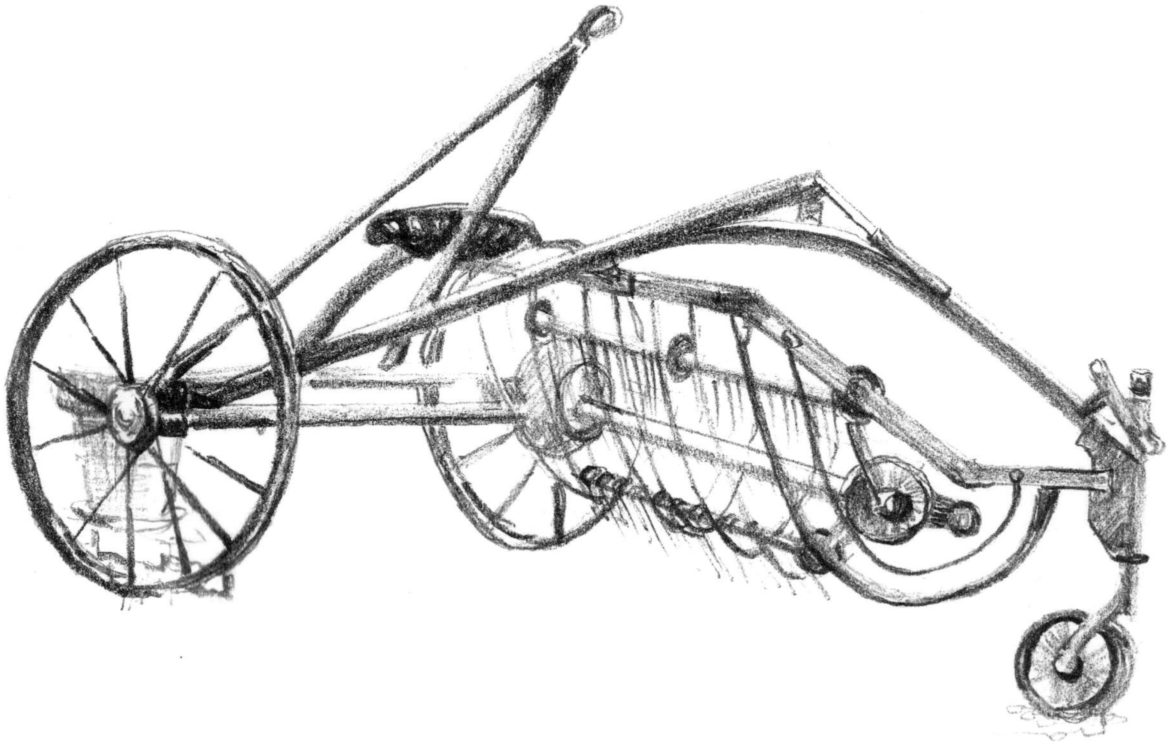

We passed through attractive Friesian countryside with long low farmhouses set to house the grazing herds of black and white cattle during the long cold winter months, well tended fields, tractors working. We noticed changes in the vegetation along the banks for all the spring flowers had given way to lush green undergrowth. Rosebay willow herb swayed in the light breeze whilst patches of yellow sow thistle and hawkweed could be seen together with the twining stems of bindweed. The banks were lined with rows of lime and aspen.

We tied up to a mooring along with several working barges and sought fresh supplies for we would now be going to sea!

Delfzijl lies on the southern bank of the Ems estuary. The Northern bank belongs to Germany. The main Ems channel was well marked, but the route leading across the Wadddenzee to the German islands was something different! The water is very shallow and the banks of sand are constantly on the move. Encouraged by a local owner who knew the water, we joined a line of craft seeking to cross to Nordeney – a line of withies tied at random with coloured string marked the channel. No deviation was possible! At the height of the tide this can be done. We had only inches of water beneath our keel!

Soon the lush farmland gave way to the industrial approaches to Delfzijl, the gateway to the sea.

North Friesland – route to the N.Sea

Chemical plants, aluminium plants and other industrial buildings lined the long protected channel that led out into the estuary. Delfzijl is the fifth largest sea port of Holland and employs a great number of people in its industries.

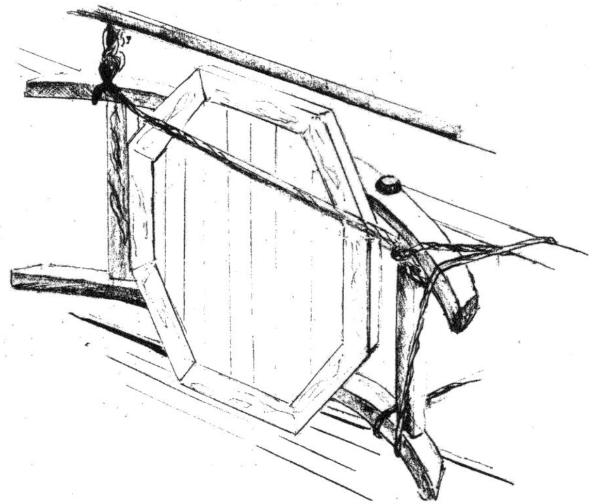

Preparations were made in readiness for passage on the open sea. Down came the canvas awning. Out came the life raft, stored conveniently in the bilges whilst we remained in inland waters.. Stowed away were lamps, cameras, binoculars and all things that might shift. Lashed down were the deck table and our chairs. Out came life jackets and safety harnesses. Lastly the dinghy was secured in the davits.

We were ready to go ... but that is another story!

Main Water Routes of Holland

Aalsmeer	44
Afsluitdijk	27
Alkmaar	29
Arcen	4
Batenburg	7
Bijland	45
Blokzijl	16
Cuijk	5
Delfzijl	42
Den Helder	28
Doesberg	37
Dordrecht	32
Enkhuizen	26
Feanen Lakes	18
Gouda	31
Heusden	8
Hindeloopen	22
Hoorn	25
Ijlst	19
Kampen	15
Kessel	2
Lemmer	21
Liege	36
Loosdrecht	12
Maasbracht	1
Maastricht	35
Maarssen	11

23	Makkum
10	Meerkerk
40	Meppel
13	Muiden
14	Naarden
43	Nordeney
41	N.Willemskanaal
6	Ravenstein
34	Rekem
17	Sneek
24	Stavoren
20	Tjeukemeer
3	Venlo
33	Weert
30	Wormeveer
9	Woudrichem
38	Zutphen
39	Zwolle

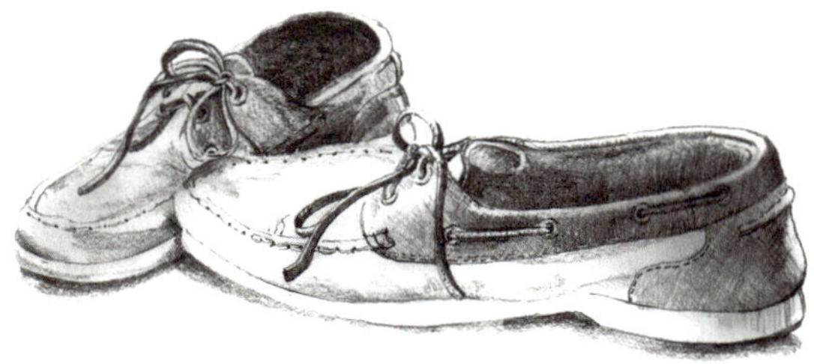

Postcript

This book has been compiled from my sketchbooks, e-mails and notes, made whilst we have made several journeys throughout the waterways of Holland. The years between school and retirement were otherwise filled – I drew little or nothing. Then came the joy of rediscovery – the pleasure of drawing now that days are unencumbered with the stress of working hours. Whilst in no way do I intend this to be a book of instruction, a few lines may be of help.

• We can all take photographs and most of us do so.
• We CAN all draw – but most of us gave up trying! - remember an image drawn will be remembered long after our photographs have become dusty memories

All that you need are:

- A few grades of pencils – HB – 2B and 4B and a good eraser
- A pad of cartridge paper or a sketchbook, available from any good stationer
- Good powers of observation!

Three of my grandchildren enjoy an outing and learn much from a short but concentrated half hour of fun.

A child will draw a house, usually a rectangle with a triangle for a roof, perhaps some simple windows, a door and a chimney. We can do better than that by observing. Do the lines of the roof go up or down as it falls further away? Look again! Try to determine the basic shapes first, and follow this by some shading. On which side does the light fall? This will help to express form. Remember that tone is more important than colour. It helps to define shape and it helps to define position – which point is furthest from your vision.?

All you need to colour your image:

- Either pans or tubes of watercolour – I suggest:
  Cadmium Yellow, RawSienna, Cadmium Red, Alizarin Crimson, French Ultramarine, Burnt Sienna, Raw Umber and Sap Green
  (Black has no place in your box – mix the three primaries to achieve this!)
- 2-3 brushes – preferably sable – in different sizes
- A pad of watercolour paper or good quality cartridge paper.

Why not have a go? Ten minutes is all you should need to make a quick sketch, perhaps half an hour if you wish to add colour.